CONTENTS

COUNT ON A CASSEROLE!

Casseroles are one of modern homemaker's favorite convenience foods, even though casserole cookery is well over 200 years old. The idea for a one-pot meal is said to have originated in France. It received its name from the French word "casse," a utensil used by European cooks in preparing stews and other large amounts of food. The "casse" sat on the back of the stove and was the receptacle for all leftover vegetables and meats creating a delicious, bubbling meal-in-a-dish.

Today, casserole ingredients have gone beyond the use of leftovers, although that is still one of the best uses. Now they can include any ingredient from the most economical to the most gourmet. Experience the real fun of cooking by making something from "nothing"—combining a bit of leftover meat, a little gravy, a cut-up baked potato and other coarsely chopped vegetables to produce something even more delectable than the original. Casseroles are the ideal vehicle for this art of creative cooking.

Casserole meals are also great time savers. The ingredients can often be combined directly in the dish, then placed into the oven and forgotten until dinner time. How perfect this is for the busy homemaker, anyone following a demanding career, or the hostess who prefers to spend time with her guests rather than in the kitchen.

Many homemakers prepare enough of every casserole recipe for two meals—one to serve now and another to freeze for later. These recipes will stir your imagination, but try your own by varying vegetables or sauces. Turn to page 121 for some new ideas, too. Before you know it, your freezer will become a casserole delicatessen!

CHOOSING CHEESE . . .

Of all the delicious cheeses available, these are the ones which blend best in casseroles. Cheese freezes well too. Natural cheese such as Swiss and Cheddar keep about 6 weeks; process cheeses about 4 months. Thaw all cheeses overnight before using and use fairly soon after thawing.

Mozzarella—semisoft white cheese—especially good in tomato-based casseroles.

Parmesan—sharp, pungent cheese—delicious in pasta casseroles.

Swiss—mild nutty flavor—elastic body that blends well with vegetables and pork.

Cheddar—firm cheese which has a mild flavor when fresh; sharp as it ages—good in all types of casseroles . . . ground beef, seafood, and pork.

Monterey Jack—a mild Cheddar type cheese made from skim milk.

Muenster—semisoft mild cheese made from whole milk.

Romano—granular, hard texture—use grated as casserole topping or lightly with Italian-type casseroles.

HERBS AND SPICES FOR CASSEROLES

Seasonings add marvelous flavor to casseroles—and bring out the full, natural flavor of every ingredient. There are three types of seasonings—herbs, spices, and natural vegetable seasonings. Herbs can be found fresh, dried, or powdered.

Which herbs do you use? If you are just beginning to experiment with herbs, we suggest that you start with the so-called "basic" herbs, those most commonly used. After you have mastered the art of using these, try your hand at herb combinations and the more unusual herbs.

Basil is a delicate and fragrant herb especially popular in tomato dishes or in those with a tomato sauce base. Its rich flavor is a nice addition to beef, veal, pork, lamb, and seafood casseroles. Try basil with vegetables, too, especially peas, string beans, potatoes, and spinach.

Chive has often been described as "toned-down onion." It tastes best when fresh. Its piquant flavor combines delightfully with beef, lamb, veal, and poultry casseroles.

Dill has a much stronger flavor than either basil or chive. It should be added near the end of cooking and is particularly good in fish and beef dishes. Use with a very light touch.

Sweet marjoram is a wonderfully versatile herb. It can be used to good advantage in all meat, fish and seafood casseroles, and in such vegetable dishes as peas, spinach, and green beans.

Thyme is always used in an herb bouquet with bay leaf. It adds an interesting flavor to beans and potatoes as well as seafood and fish casseroles. And it goes well with beef, game, lamb, veal, and pork. It is indispensable in Creole dishes. Use sparingly.

Oregano has enjoyed renewed popularity in the United States, thanks in part to the enthusiasm for Italian cookery. It is often used with tomato-based dishes in combination with basil.

Sage has a powerful flavor and should be used with a very light touch. It is a vital ingredient in stuffings and is particularly good with mild-flavored meat dishes, such as those made with pork, veal, or poultry.

Mint is one of the most popular herbs. Add dried mint leaves to cooked foods shortly before cooking time is up. It is excellent in most lamb dishes and brings an exciting flavor note to peas, carrots, and snap beans.

Bay leaf is used in herb bouquets with thyme. It is cooked for a short time with the dish and is removed before serving. It has a bitter taste if eaten. Bay leaf brings a tempting flavor to hearty meat casseroles, especially those made of beef.

These basic spices can be used to add new life to your casserole cookery.

Caraway, a seed most often used in bread and cake making, is also a flavorful addition to beet casseroles or those made with potatoes or cabbage.

Cayenne is ground from the seeds and pods of various peppers. This spice should be used with a very light touch. It accents the natural flavors of savory dishes—those with spicy sauces or those made from meats which have been marinated. Try it with a meat pie for a real flavor treat.

Curry powder is a combination of eight or ten spices ground together. It has a very sharp flavor and is used most often in Indian cooking. If you want to experiment, try it with poultry, seafood, fish casseroles, or those made with vegetables or rice. One warning: curry powder scorches and changes flavor when cooked at high temperature. Keep the temperature as low as possible.

Paprika, the ground powder of the pepper plant, is a favorite mild-flavored spice. It adds color to pale meat dishes and to fish casseroles. Its mild flavor highlights casseroles made of fish, poultry, pork, or veal.

Allspice is most often used in combination with other spices in fruit dishes and desserts. But try just a touch of it in your next beef casserole or meat pie. You'll be delighted with the results!

Seasonings do not have to be limited to the usual herbs and spices. For thousands of years, cooks have used vegetables for their seasoning value. Foremost among the seasoning vegetables are the various *Onions.* Scallions add a piquant flavor to sauces. Onions, used in moderation, are a delicious flavor note in almost every casserole.

Try a few **Mushrooms** in your next casserole—they have a distinct flavor which perks up every dish.

And **Celery** is a real bonus! Chop a few celery stalks and add them to your next tomato-based dish. Add chopped leaves to cauliflower, cheese, or game dishes. Your family will applaud!

Many of the seasonings mentioned here are available in a salt form. The presence of a salt base may change the flavor of any seasoning and make it rancid. Use seasoning salts with care, and taste as you go.

As you become accustomed to experimenting with herbs and spices, you and your family will begin to discover great flavor treats awaiting you. A skillful touch of seasoning turns a casserole of leftovers into a family-pleasing treat. Try it for yourself and see!

FREEZING CASSEROLES

Preparing . . .

- To keep the casserole dish in circulation, line with foil before filling. Freeze, then remove frozen mixture from dish. Wrap, being sure package is airtight. Remove foil and replace in original container for baking.
- Date each package. Most casseroles can be safely frozen for 3 to 4 months: vegetable casseroles up to 6 months; casseroles with fatty sauce only 2 months.
- Season with caution before freezing: onion, salt, and chili powder weaken during freezing; cloves, pepper, garlic, and celery become stronger when frozen.

Thawing . . .

- Allow a frozen casserole mixture to thaw in refrigerator before cooking. Add an extra 15 to 20 minutes baking time.
- Undercook a mixture to be frozen, so it won't overcook as it's reheated.
- Do not include much fat in a freezer mixture. It may become rancid in about 2 months.
- If microwave is used, thaw and cook in one continuous process. Allow one-third to one-half more time for the defrosting process.

Do's and Don'ts . . .

- Don't freeze mixtures with hard-boiled egg whites (unless first put through a sieve), mayonnaise, sour cream or raw vegetables.
- Do add toppings such as cheese or crumbs after thawing.
- Don't freeze pastry; it will become soggy.
- Don't freeze salad greens, raw vegetables, potatoes, and fried foods; they should be added just before reheating.
- Do remember: casseroles baked in a deep dish require more cooking time than those in a shallow one.

Beef and Veal

Beef and Dumpling Bake

2 lb. round steak, cubed
1/3 c. flour
2 med. onions, sliced
2 bay leaves
1 4-oz. can sliced mushrooms
1 can cream of chicken soup
1 can onion soup
1 tbsp. Worcestershire sauce
1 10-oz. package frozen peas
4 green pepper rings
1/2 c. chopped ripe olives
Parsley Dumplings

Coat steak with flour. Brown in small amount of shortening in skillet. Add onions, bay leaves, mushrooms, soups and 1 soup can water. Cover. Bake at 400 degrees for 1 1/2 hours. Remove bay leaves. Add peas, green pepper and olives. Drop dumplings by rounded tea-spoonfuls over steak mixture. Cover. Bake for 25 minutes longer.

Parsley Dumplings

1 egg
1/3 c. milk
2 tbsp. parsley flakes
2 tbsp. oil
1/4 tsp. sage
1 c. flour
1 1/2 tsp. baking powder
1/2 tsp. salt

Combine egg, milk, parsley flakes, oil and sage in bowl; mix well. Combine flour, baking powder and salt; add to egg mixture. Stir until just mixed.

Margie Carrington
Newport News, Virginia

Beef Curry-in-a-Hurry

1 1/2 lb. boneless beef
1/2 c. chopped onion
1 clove of garlic, minced
3 tbsp. butter
1 to 1 1/2 tbsp. curry powder
1 tsp. salt
1/2 c. golden raisins
1 tbsp. flour
1 med. apple, peeled, sliced
1 pkg. frozen peas and carrots, thawed
1 10-oz. package corn bread mix
1 c. cubed Cheddar cheese

Cut beef into 1/2-inch cubes. Saute onion and garlic in butter in large skillet until tender. Add beef. Cook until browned. Combine curry, salt and 1 1/2 cups water. Add to skillet with raisins. Simmer, covered, for 20 minutes or until beef is tender. Blend flour into 1/4 cup water until smooth. Stir into beef mixture gradually. Bring to a boil, stirring constantly. Add apple. Pour into 2-quart casserole. Arrange peas and carrots over top. Prepare corn bread, using package directions. Fold in cheese. Spoon over top of casserole in diagonal strips. Bake at 425 degrees for 12 to 15 minutes. Yield: 8 servings.

Picture for this recipe on page 9.

Beef Pilau

1 lb. round steak, cubed
1 lg. onion, finely chopped
2 tsp. salt
2 tbsp. butter
1 c. quick-cooking rice
1 20-oz. can tomatoes
1 20-oz. can red kidney beans
1 can beef consomme
1 tsp. chili powder
1/4 tsp. oregano

Brown steak and onion with salt in butter in skillet. Alternate layers of beef mixture, rice, tomatoes and beans in 2-quart casserole until all ingredients are used. Combine remaining ingredients in bowl; mix well. Pour over layers. Bake at 350 degrees for 1 hour.

Elese Nichols
Ely, Nevada

Chopped Beef with Yorkshire Pudding

1 c. flour
Salt to taste
1 c. milk
2 eggs
Freshly grated nutmeg
Dash of cayenne pepper
Dash of mace
1 1/2 lb. finely chopped beef
1 1/2 tbsp. grated onion
1 tsp. finely chopped parsley
1 tsp. chives
1/2 clove of garlic, finely chopped
Pepper to taste
Pinch of cloves

Sift flour and salt in bowl. Add milk gradually, stirring constantly, until smooth. Add eggs, one at a time, beating well after each addition. Season with nutmeg, cayenne pepper and mace; beat thoroughly. Set aside. Combine next 7 ingredients with salt in bowl; mix well. Heat well-greased large shallow baking pan in 450-degree oven until sizzling. Pour in ½ of the batter. Spread on beef mixture quickly, using a wet spatula. Pour remaining batter over beef. Bake until pudding rises and begins to brown. Reduce temperature to 350 degrees. Bake for 20 minutes longer or until pudding leaves sides of pan. Serve with rich tomato sauce or mushroom sauce.

Shirley Belyea
Alberta, Canada

Priest's Lunch

3 lb. beef brisket, cubed
4 potatotes, peeled, diced
1 c. diced celery
8 sm. white onions
3 tomatoes, quartered
4 tbsp. chopped parsley
3 cloves of garlic, minced
1 tsp. salt
2 tbsp. paprika
4 bay leaves
12 whole peppercorns
2 cans consomme

Combine all ingredients with 2½ consomme cans water in deep casserole. Cover tightly. Bake at 350 degrees for 2½ hours.

Judy Angel
Farnsworth, New Hampshire

Cheddar Beef

1 lb. round steak, cubed
½ c. chopped onion
1 c. diced celery
4 or 5 lg. potatoes, sliced
½ c. grated Cheddar cheese
1 can cream of mushroom soup
Salt and pepper to taste

Saute steak and onion in skillet until brown. Add celery and ½ cup water. Simmer until tender-crisp. Alternate layers of potatoes and steak mixture, sprinkling each layer with cheese. Blend soup and seasonings with ½ soup can water in small bowl. Pour over mixture. Bake at 350 degrees for 1½ hours.

Linda Larsen
Portland, Maine

Heritage Casserole

1½ lb. beef steak, cubed
3 tbsp. oil
½ c. chopped onion
3 c. cooked rice
½ c. sour cream
1 tsp. salt
½ c. catsup
1 c. cottage cheese
½ c. chopped sweet pickle
¼ tsp. pepper
1 c. grated Cheddar cheese

Cook beef in hot oil in skillet until lightly browned on all sides; add onion. Simmer, covered, for about 20 minutes. Drain. Add remaining ingredients except cheese, blending thoroughly. Turn into buttered 2-quart casserole. Sprinkle with cheese. Bake in 350-degree oven for 25 minutes. Yield: 8 servings.

Patricia Langston
Alamosa, Colorado

Peasant Casserole

2 lb. top beef sirloin, cubed
4 tbsp. butter
1½ c. thinly sliced onions
1¼ tsp. salt
½ tsp. pepper
¼ tsp. nutmeg
4 c. seasoned mashed potatoes
2 c. thinly sliced apples
2 tbsp. bread crumbs

Brown beef in 2 tablespoons butter in skillet. Remove. Saute onions in pan drippings until tender. Stir in salt, pepper and nutmeg. Alternate layers of potatoes, beef, apples and onions in greased 2-quart casserole, ending with potatoes. Sprinkle with bread crumbs. Dot with remaining butter. Bake at 375 degrees for 25 minutes. Yield: 4-6 servings.

Sharon Stern
Williston, North Dakota

Club-Day Casserole

3 lb. beef stew meat, cubed
1½ c. flour
1½ tsp. seasoned salt
½ tsp. pepper
½ c. oil
1 pkg. dry onion soup mix
1 tbsp. mushroom powder
½ tsp. marjoram
1 tbsp. Worcestershire sauce
2 tsp. parsley flakes
3 c. prepared biscuit mix
4 tbsp. butter
1 c. milk

Coat beef cubes with flour mixed with seasoned salt and pepper. Reserve flour mixture. Brown beef in oil in skillet. Add 2 cups water and next 5 ingredients; mix well. Simmer, covered, for 1 hour. Blend 4 tablespoons reserved flour mixture with 1 cup water in small bowl. Add to skillet. Cook until thickened, stirring constantly. Pour into greased 9 × 13-inch baking dish. Combine biscuit mix, butter and milk following package directions. Cover beef mixture with biscuit rounds. Bake at 400 degrees for 20 minutes or until brown.

Susan Dale
Minot, North Dakota

Magic Meat and Rice

¾ c. rice
1 tsp. salt
1 lb. beef, cubed
1 lb. lean pork, cubed
2 tbsp. shortening
1 c. diced celery
¼ c. chopped green pepper
½ c. chopped onion
1 can cream of mushroom soup
1 can chicken noodle soup
5 tsp. soy sauce

Place rice in greased 2-quart casserole. Add 2 cups boiling water and salt; set aside. Brown beef and pork slowly in hot shortening in skillet. Arrange over rice; add vegetables. Stir in soups and soy sauce. Bake at 325 degrees for 2 hours. Yield: 6-8 servings.

Dorothy Smith
Virginia, Illinois

Oven Beef Stew

1½ lb. beef, cubed
12 to 16 sm. white onions
3 med. carrots, sliced ¼ in. thick
1 10-oz. package frozen green peas,
    thawed
1 tbsp. flour
2 tbsp. tomato sauce
1 bay leaf
1 tbsp. red wine vinegar
⅛ tsp. thyme
1½ tsp. salt
1 clove of garlic
⅛ tsp. pepper

Brown beef in skillet; reserve drippings. Layer beef, onions, carrots and peas in 2-quart casserole. Mix reserved drippings with remaining ingredients and 1½ cups water. Pour over vegetables and beef. Bake, covered, in 350-degree oven for 1¾ hours or until beef and vegetables are tender. Yield: 8 servings.

June Fletcher
Litchfield, Illinois

Southern Casserole Pie

1 lb. stew meat
Flour
Salt and pepper to taste
Garlic salt to taste
Oregano to taste
2 med. potatoes, chopped
1 can whole tomatoes
1 can peas and carrots
1 onion, chopped
¼ head cabbage, shredded
1 recipe biscuits

Coat stew meat in flour and seasoning. Saute meat in skillet until brown. Combine meat and vegetables in casserole. Add enough water to cover. Bake, covered, at 350 degrees for 1½ hours or until tender. Uncover. Drop 8 biscuits on top of stew. Bake at 400 degrees for 10 minutes or until biscuits are brown.

Sue Slusser
Agra, Oklahoma

Stay-Abed Stew

1 can tomato soup
2 lb. stew beef, cubed
1 can peas

1 c. sliced carrots
2 onions, chopped
1 tsp. salt
Dash of pepper
1 lg. potato, sliced

Combine all ingredients in casserole with ½ soup can water; mix well. Bake, covered, at 275 degrees for 5 hours. Yield: 8 servings.

Marilyn Kay Clark
Curtis, Nebraska

Steak Hot Dish

1½ lb. round steak, cubed
2 med. onions, chopped
2 tbsp. shortening
1 can mushroom soup
1 can mushrooms
2 cans chicken rice soup
2 c. chopped celery
1 c. rice
Salt and pepper to taste

Brown steak and onions in shortening in skillet. Add ½ cup water. Simmer for 1 hour. Mix remaining ingredients with 2 cups water in bowl. Combine steak and onions with soup mixture in 4-quart baking dish. Bake at 350 degrees for 1½ to 2 hours, stirring occasionally. Yield: 6 servings.

Linda Ahrendt
Moorhead, Iowa

Stroganoff Casserole

1 lb. round steak, cubed
1 lg. onion, sliced
Salt and pepper to taste
Green pepper (opt.)
1 can mushroom soup
1 c. sour cream
Olives (opt.)
1 8-oz. package macaroni, cooked

Brown steak and onions in a small amount of shortening in skillet. Add salt, pepper, green pepper and soup. Simmer for 10 minutes. Remove from heat. Stir in sour cream, olives and macaroni. Spoon into greased casserole. Bake at 350 degrees for 45 minutes.

Constance Cebulla
Staples, Minnesota

Surprise Casserole

1 2-lb. sirloin tip, cubed
2 tbsp. onion, minced
1 tbsp. butter
1 3-oz. can whole mushrooms
1 bay leaf
1 tsp. Worcestershire sauce
2 c. cooked wide noodles
½ c. evaporated milk
1 tsp. salt
¼ c. Cheddar cheese
1 c. croutons
2 tbsp. pimento strips

Saute steak and onion in 1 tablespoon butter in skillet until lightly browned. Add liquid from mushrooms, bay leaf and Worcestershire sauce. Cover. Simmer for 30 minutes or until meat is tender. Remove bay leaf. Combine steak and drippings with noodles, milk, salt and ½ cup water in greased casserole. Sprinkle with cheese and croutons. Bake at 325 degrees for 1 hour. Garnish with pimento. Yield: 4-6 servings.

Dorothy Scothoin
Kennedy, Minnesota

Leftover Spaghetti Casserole

1 onion, minced
½ c. celery, chopped
4 tbsp. butter
1 tbsp. flour
½ c. milk
2 c. leftover roast beef, cubed
3 c. cooked spaghetti
1 sm. can mushrooms
1 c. tomato sauce
1 tsp. Worcestershire sauce
Grated cheese

Saute onion and celery in butter in skillet until tender. Blend in flour. Stir in milk. Cook until thick stirring constantly. Add remaining ingredients except cheese. Pour into casserole. Top with cheese. Bake at 350 degrees for 25 minutes. Yield: 6-8 servings.

Doris Gruber
Walsh, Colorado

Weekend Casserole

1 lb. beef chuck, cubed
½ c. Burgundy
1 can condensed consomme
¾ tsp. salt
⅛ tsp. pepper
1 med. onion, sliced
¼ c. flour
¼ c. fine dry bread crumbs

Combine beef, wine, consomme, salt, pepper and onion in casserole. Mix flour with bread crumbs; stir into casserole mixture. Cover. Bake at 300 degrees for 3 hours or until beef is tender. Serve over rice, noodles or mashed potatoes. Yield: 4 servings.

Mary A. Lambert
Lemoore, California

Friendship Meat Pie

2 c. diced cooked beef
2 c. white sauce
1 c. cooked mixed vegetables
1 onion, minced
1 tsp. Worcestershire sauce
Salt and pepper to taste
1 recipe pie pastry

Combine all ingredients except pastry in casserole; mix well. Roll out pastry on floured surface. Place on top of casserole. Bake at 425 degrees for ½ hour. Yield: 4 servings.

Mrs. J. E. Robertson
Friendship, Tennessee

Original Beef-Macaroni Casserole

1 med. onion, diced
1 stalk of celery, chopped
2 tbsp. butter
2 c. cooked beef, cubed
1 c. macaroni, cooked
1 can tomato soup
Salt to taste
2 tbsp. grated cheese

Saute onion and celery in butter in skillet for 5 minutes. Add beef; brown lightly. Add remaining ingredients except cheese; mix well. Pour into casserole. Top with cheese. Bake at 350 degrees until bubbly.

Nadine Elder
Warsaw, Ohio

Roast Beef Casserole

4 med. potatoes, cut into ½-in. cubes
1 beef bouillon cube
4 med. carrots, diced
1 med. onion, minced
1 green pepper, diced
½ c. catsup
Salt and pepper to taste
1 c. diced roast beef

Boil potatoes for 3 minutes in salted water in saucepan; drain, reserving water. Add bouillon cube to 1 cup reserved potato water in saucepan. Bring to a boil; add vegetables. Cook for 5 minutes; add catsup. Combine all ingredients in 2-quart casserole with enough extra catsup and reserved potato water to just cover, if necessary. Bake, covered, at 350 degrees for ½ hour. Remove cover. Bake for ½ hour longer. Yield: 6-8 servings.

Margaret H. Meetze
Heath Springs, South Carolina

Rigatoni Special

2 to 3 c. finely chopped cooked roast
    beef
1 lg. onion, minced
2 med. cloves of garlic, minced
1 egg
Salt and pepper to taste
1 pkg. rigatoni noodles, cooked
1 can tomato soup
2 cans enchilada sauce

Combine first 6 ingredients in bowl; mix well. Stuff cooled rigatoni with mixture. Place in lightly greased casserole. Combine soup and enchilada sauce. Pour over stuffed rigatoni. Bake at 350 degrees for 30 minutes. Yield: 6-8 servings.

Connie Bullock
Kalamazoo, Michigan

Chuck Roast Supreme

3 lb. chuck roast
2 tbsp. Worcestershire sauce
1 pkg. dried onion soup mix
1 can mushroom soup
Potatoes
Carrots
Parsnips
Sm. whole onions

Place roast in casserole. Sprinkle Worcestershire sauce and onion soup mix over roast. Add mushroom soup. Place desired amount of vegetables around roast. Bake, covered, at 350 degrees for 2½ hours or until roast is tender. Yield: 6 servings.

Janet Daily
Grove City, Ohio

Flank Steak Casserole

2 lb. flank steak, scored
2 tbsp. salad oil
1 clove of garlic, minced
1 sm. lemon, thinly sliced
4 whole cloves
2 beef bouillon cubes
2⅔ c. instant rice
½ c. sliced stuffed olives
2 lg. peeled tomatoes, thickly sliced

Brown steak in oil in skillet. Add next 4 ingredients and 1 cup water. Simmer, covered, for 1 to 2 hours. Strain pan drippings. Add enough water to measure 3 cups liquid. Pour into saucepan. Bring to a boil; stir in rice. Cover and remove from heat; let stand for 13 minutes. Toss rice with olives. Pour into 3-quart casserole. Place steak on rice. Top with tomato slices. Bake, covered, at 350 degrees for 30 minutes.

Mary Weaver
Schwenksville, Pennsylvania

Meal-In-One Casserole

1 lb. round steak, ¼ in. thick
2 tsp. salt
1 tsp. paprika
2½ tbsp. flour
2 tbsp. shortening
1½ onions, sliced
3 potatoes, thinly sliced
1 c. canned tomatoes
½ tsp. sugar
1 tbsp. catsup

Cut steak into 4 pieces. Combine 1 teaspoon salt, paprika and flour. Coat steak with flour mixture. Brown in shortening in skillet. Layer steak, onions and potatoes in casserole. Combine remaining ingredients with 1 teaspoon salt; mix well. Pour over casserole. Bake, covered, at 350 degrees for 1½ hours, adding small amounts of water or red wine to prevent dryness.

Sandra Williams
Wilmington, Delaware

Mom's Swiss Steak

1 c. flour
1½ lb. steak
Salt and pepper to taste
1 lg. onion, chopped
2 tbsp. cooking oil
8 carrots, sliced
1 No. 2 can tomatoes

Pound flour into steak using tenderizing mallet. Season both sides with salt and pepper. Saute onion in oil in skillet. Add steak. Brown on both sides. Place meat and onion in casserole; add carrots. Beat tomatoes with electric mixer. Pour over carrots. Bake, covered, in 350-degree oven for 1½ hours.

Jerrie L. Evans
Caldwell, Idaho

Round Steak Supper

2 lb. round steak, 1 in. thick
2 tsp. salt
Dash of pepper
Flour
6 med. onions, sliced
¼ c. shortening
3 lg. potatoes, halved
1 can tomato soup
1 1-lb. can French-cut green beans

Cut round steak into serving pieces; season with salt and pepper. Roll in flour. Saute onions in hot shortening in skillet until tender; remove. Brown steak pieces slowly on both sides. Place in 3-quart casserole. Add onions and potatoes; pour soup over top. Bake, covered, in 350-degree oven for 1¾ hours or until steak is tender. Add green beans. Bake for 10 minutes longer. Yield: 6-8 servings.

Sue Kidd
Odessa, Texas

Judith's Steak Casserole

1 lb. cube steak
Flour
Salt and pepper to taste
2 tbsp. melted shortening
1 pkg. dry onion soup mix
½ c. rice

Coat steak with flour; season to taste. Arrange steak in shortening in baking dish. Bake at 400 degrees until brown. Reduce temperature to 350 degrees. Sprinkle soup mix over steak. Add rice and 1¼ cups water. Bake, covered, for 1 hour or until meat and rice are tender. Yield: 4 servings.

Judith Jones
Richlands, North Carolina

Swiss Steak with Olive-Tomato Sauce

1 2-lb. round steak, 1 in. thick
½ c. flour
1½ tsp. salt
½ tsp. pepper
3 tbsp. shortening
2 med. onions, sliced
½ c. sliced pimento-stuffed olives
2 16-oz. cans tomatoes
1 tbsp. bottled thick meat sauce
1 bay leaf
1 tsp. light brown sugar
⅛ tsp. thyme leaves

Cut steak into serving pieces. Combine flour, salt and pepper; pound into steak with tenderizing mallet or edge of saucer. Heat shortening in large skillet. Add steak; saute until well browned on both sides. Arrange in large, shallow baking dish; place onion rings and olives over steak. Combine tomatoes, meat sauce, bay leaf, brown sugar and thyme leaves in saucepan; mix well. Bring to a boil, breaking up tomatoes with back of spoon. Pour over steak; cover. Bake in 350-degree oven for 1½ hours or until steak is fork tender. Skim off excess fat before serving. Yield: 6 servings.

Amy Lee
Sarasota, Florida

Stuffed Cubed Steaks

4 cubed steaks
2 tbsp. flour
Dash of pepper
½ tsp. salt
1 c. soft bread crumbs
¼ tsp. poultry seasoning
1 tsp. minced onion
2 tbsp. margarine, melted
⅓ c. rice, cooked
2½ c. canned tomatoes
2 tbsp. butter

Coat steaks with flour seasoned with pepper and ¼ teaspoon salt. Combine next 4 ingredients with 2 tablespoons water, in bowl; mix well. Spread each steak with ¼ of bread crumb mixture. Fold over; fasten with toothpick. Place in greased shallow baking dish; arrange rice around steak. Add tomatoes and remaining salt; dot with butter. Bake, covered, at 350 degrees for 1 hour or until steaks are tender.

Elizabeth H. Davis
Waterford, Pennsylvania

Elegant Beef

1 clove of garlic, minced
½ c. chopped onion
2 tbsp. shortening
1 lb. sirloin, cut into 2-in. strips
½ tsp. salt
⅛ tsp. pepper
¼ c. flour
1 3-oz. can sliced mushrooms
2 tbsp. catsup
½ to 1 c. beef bouillon
½ c. sour cream
Cooked wide noodles
Poppy seed to taste

Saute garlic and onion in shortening in skillet. Dredge beef with seasoned flour. Add to onion mixture. Brown lightly. Add mushrooms, catsup and ½ cup bouillon. Simmer, covered, for 30 minutes, adding more bouillon as needed. Add sour cream. Simmer for 30 minutes. Alternate layers of beef mixture and noodles in casserole. Refrigerate, covered, overnight. Sprinkle with poppy seed. Bake at 325 degrees for 30 minutes, adding more bouillon if necessary. Yield: 6 servings.

Sissy Lang
Huntsville, Alabama

Man-Style Casserole

1½ c. beef, cut into strips
½ c. thinly sliced onion
2 tbsp. butter
1 c. cream of celery soup
⅓ c. milk
1 c. shredded cheese
Dash of pepper
3 c. sliced cooked potatoes
Paprika

Saute beef with onion in butter in saucepan until tender. Blend soup, milk, ¾ cup cheese and pepper in bowl. Arrange layers of potatoes, beef mixture and sauce in 1½-quart casserole. Sprinkle top with remaining cheese and paprika. Bake at 375 degrees for 30 minutes.

Pat Willoughby
Hamlin, Texas

Peppered Tenderloin Casserole

2 lb. boneless beef tenderloin
4 tbsp. margarine
2 tbsp. olive oil
1 tsp. salt
½ tsp. coarsely ground pepper
Dash of ground sage
Dash of ground cumin
1 lb. mushrooms, quartered
2 med. green peppers, chopped
2 cloves of garlic, finely chopped
1 med. onion, cut into wedges
2 med. tomatoes, cut into wedges
½ c. soy sauce
2 tbsp. cider vinegar
2 tbsp. tomato paste

Slice beef into ¼-inch wide strips. Saute in 2 tablespoons margarine and 1 tablespoon oil in large skillet. Place in baking dish. Sprinkle with salt, pepper, sage and cumin; toss lightly. Saute mushrooms in remaining margarine and oil in skillet for 2 minutes. Add to casserole. Stir green peppers, garlic and onion into pan drippings. Saute for 2 minutes. Add to casserole. Arrange tomatoes on top. Combine remaining ingredients in skillet. Heat to boiling point, stirring constantly. Pour over beef mixture; toss lightly. Bake, covered, in 350 degree oven for 30 minutes. Yield: 6 servings.

Audrey Swanson
Tinley Park, Illinois

Ruth's Steak Casserole

1 lb. round steak
6 med. potatoes, sliced
2 med. onions, sliced
4 carrots, sliced
1 can tomato soup
2 tbsp. Worcestershire sauce
½ tsp. salt

Cut steak into strips. Layer vegetables and steak in greased casserole. Add next 3 ingredients. Bake at 350 for 1 hour. Yield: 6 servings.

Ruth Jennings
Eufaula, Alabama

Alene's Veal Casserole

⅓ c. flour
1 tsp. paprika
2 lb. veal round steak, cubed
¼ c. shortening
1¾ c. cooked onions
2 cans cream of chicken soup

Mix flour and paprika; pound into veal. Saute in shortening in skillet. Place in casserole. Add onions, 1½ cans soup and 1½ soup cans water; mix well. Bake at 350 degrees for 45 minutes.

Dumplings

2 c. flour
2 tsp. baking powder
½ tsp. salt
1 tsp. poultry seasoning
1 tsp. poppy seed
1 tsp. onion flakes
¼ c. salad oil
1 c. milk
¼ c. melted butter
1 c. bread crumbs
1 c. sour cream

Sift dry ingredients, except bread crumbs; add seasonings. Blend oil and milk; lightly stir into dry ingredients. Combine butter and crumbs; drop dumplings into crumb mixture. Drop dumplings on top of casserole. Bake at 425 degrees for 20 to 25 minutes. Heat remaining soup and sour cream; serve with casserole. Yield: 8 servings.

Jean Cummings
Kingsford, Michigan

Ruth's Veal Casserole

1/4 lb. beef, chopped
1 lb. veal, chopped
1 tbsp. oil
1 onion, minced
1/2 c. rice
1 can mushroom soup
1 can cream of chicken soup
Dash of paprika
1/2 tsp. salt
1 sm. can mushrooms
1/2 c. slivered almonds

Brown beef and veal in oil in skillet. Add onions; brown lightly. Stir in remaining ingredients except almonds with 2 1/4 cups water. Pour into casserole. Bake at 350 degrees for 1 1/2 hours, stirring occasionally. Top with almonds. Bake until brown. Yield: 6-8 servings.

Ruth DeFriese
Knoxville, Tennessee

Veal Hot Dish

1 lb. veal steak, cubed
3 tbsp. butter
3 med. onions, sliced
1 1/2 c. diced celery
1/2 c. rice
1 sm. can mushrooms
1/4 green pepper, diced
3 tbsp. soy sauce
1 can mushroom soup
1 can chicken-rice soup
1/2 tsp. salt
Pepper to taste
1/2 c. salted chopped almonds

Saute veal in butter in skillet until brown. Set veal aside. Saute onions in pan drippings until tender. Add veal and remaining ingredients except almonds, with 2 soup cans water; mix well. Spoon into baking dish. Bake at 350 degrees for 1 hour. Sprinkle with almonds. Bake for 30 minutes longer.

Joan Erickson
St. Paul, Minnesota

Veal and Potato Casserole

1 lb. boneless veal, cubed
5 tbsp. butter
4 med. potatoes, cubed
4 med. onions, coarsely chopped
1 sm. clove of garlic, minced
1/2 tsp. each salt, pepper, oregano
2 tsp. minced parsley
1 No. 2 can tomatoes
2 tbsp. cornstarch

Saute veal in butter in skillet until brown. Add potatoes, onions and garlic; brown lightly. Add seasonings, parsley and tomatoes. Blend cornstarch with 2 tablespoons cold water in small bowl. Add to skillet. Simmer for 5 minutes, stirring constantly. Pour into casserole. Bake, covered, at 325 degrees for 40 to 45 minutes until meat and vegetables are tender.

Sister Mary Benedict Beehler
Crookston, Minnesota

Veal Baked in Sour Cream

1 1/2 lb. boneless veal, cubed
1 1/2 tbsp. butter
1 tbsp. chopped onion
1/2 lb. sliced mushrooms
1 tbsp. flour
3 tbsp. water
3/4 c. sour cream
1/2 tsp. salt
1/8 tsp. pepper

Brown veal in butter in skillet; transfer to baking dish. Saute the onion and mushrooms in skillet. Stir in flour, water, sour cream, salt and pepper. Pour mushroom sauce over veal. Cover. Bake in 250-degree oven for 1 hour.

Georgia Brazil
Franklin, Tennessee

Thelma's Veal Casserole

1 lb. cubed veal
Flour
2 tbsp. shortening
1 1/2 c. sliced celery
2 sm. onions, chopped
1 can cream of chicken soup
1 can cream of mushroom soup
2 to 3 tbsp. soy sauce
1/2 c. rice

Coat veal with flour. Brown in shortening in skillet over medium heat. Stir in remaining ingredients with 1 to 1 1/2 soup cans water; mix well. Pour into 2-quart baking dish. Bake, covered, for 1 1/2 hours. Yield: 6 servings.

Thelma Ash
Hampton, Virginia

Ground Beef

Beef Bake with Cheese Biscuits

1 lb. ground beef
½ c. pork sausage
½ c. dry bread crumbs
2 tbsp. chopped onion
1 tsp. chili powder
⅛ tsp. pepper
1⅓ c. evaporated milk
1 can cream of mushroom soup
1 can cream of celery soup
1 Recipe Cheese Biscuits

Combine first 6 ingredients with ⅓ cup milk in bowl; mix well. Shape into balls. Saute in skillet. Cover. Cook for 10 minutes. Place in 2½-quart casserole. Heat soups, remaining milk and ½ cup water. Pour over meat balls. Top with Chili-Cheese Biscuits. Bake at 400 degrees for 20 to 30 minutes. Yield: 8 servings.

Cheese Biscuits

1⅓ c. sifted flour
3 tsp. baking powder
½ tsp. chili powder
¼ tsp. salt
⅓ c. shortening
1 egg, beaten
⅓ c. evaporated milk
1½ c. grated American cheese

Sift dry ingredients into bowl. Cut in shortening until crumbly. Combine egg and milk; add to dry ingredients, stirring until dough clings together. Knead lightly on floured surface. Roll out to 12-inch square. Sprinkle with cheese. Roll as for jelly roll. Cut into eight slices. Place on top of casserole.

Genia Thames
Townsend, Tennessee

Biscuit and Beef Casserole

1½ lb. ground beef
1 c. chopped onions
¼ c. milk
1 can cream of mushroom soup
1 8-oz package cream cheese, softened
1 tsp. salt
¼ c. catsup
1 can biscuits

Saute beef and onions in skillet until brown. Drain. Combine milk, soup and cream cheese in bowl. Add salt, catsup and beef; mix well. Pour into 2-quart casserole. Bake at 375 degrees for 10 minutes. Place biscuits on top. Bake for 15 to 20 minutes longer or until biscuits are golden brown. Yield: 5-6 servings.

Nancy A. Menninger
Miamisburg, Ohio

Hamburger Pie

½ lb. ground beef
¾ c. chopped onion
¾ c. chopped celery
¼ c. chopped green pepper
½ can tomato soup
1 tsp. barbecue sauce
½ tsp. salt
Dash of pepper
2 c. biscuit mix
⅔ c. milk
1 tbsp. chopped parsley
½ tsp. celery seed

Saute ground beef in skillet until brown. Add onion, celery and green pepper. Cook until onion is golden. Stir in soup, barbecue sauce, salt and pepper. Turn into 8-inch round 1½-inch deep pan. Combine biscuit mix and milk. Stir in parsley and celery seed. Roll out on floured surface into circle to fit pan. Arrange over beef mixture. Bake in 450-degree oven for 15 minutes. Yield: 6 servings.

Eloise Guerrant
Robert Lee, Texas

Bean-Macaroni Casserole

1 lb. ground beef
¼ c. minced onion
2 tsp. salt
1 No. 2 can kidney beans
1 No. 2 can tomatoes
1 7-oz. package elbow macaroni, cooked
4 slices crisp-cooked bacon, crumbled
½ lb. American cheese, grated

Saute ground beef with onion and salt in skillet until onion is clear. Add beans and tomatoes; mix well. Alternate layers of macaroni and ground beef mixture in greased 2-quart casserole until all ingredients are used. Top with bacon and cheese. Bake at 350 degrees for 30 to 40 minutes until brown. Yield: 8-10 servings.

Madge Tapp
Dixon, Kentucky

Casserole for a Crowd

1½ lb. ground beef
1 c. chopped onions
1 12-oz. can whole kernel corn, drained
1 can cream of mushroom soup
1 can cream of chicken soup
1 c. sour cream
¼ c. chopped pimento
¾ tsp. salt
½ tsp. monosodium glutamate
¼ tsp. pepper
3 c. cooked macaroni
1 c. bread crumbs, toasted
1 stick margarine, melted

Saute ground beef in skillet until crumbly. Add onions. Cook until tender. Stir in next 9 ingredients; mix well. Pour into 2 greased 2-quart casseroles. Toss crumbs and butter together. Sprinkle over casseroles. Bake at 350 degrees for 20 minutes. Yield: 12 servings.

Imogene Crawford
Flat Rock, North Carolina

Polly's Goulash

2 lb. ground beef
1 8-oz. pkg. shell macaroni, cooked
3 onions, chopped
1 green pepper, chopped
3 cloves of garlic, minced
1 8-oz. can tomato paste
1 12-oz. can yellow corn
1 3-oz. can mushrooms
1 c. grated sharp cheese
1 tbsp. brown sugar
1 tbsp. Worcestershire sauce
1 tbsp. chili powder
2 tsp. salt
¼ tsp. pepper
1 c. Sherry

Brown ground beef in skillet stirring until crumbly. Add remaining ingredients; mix well. Pour into two 1½-quart casseroles. Refrigerate overnight. Bake, covered, at 350 degrees for 1 hour.

Pauline Slate
Emporia, Virginia

Mock Ravioli

1½ lb. ground beef
3 lg. onions, finely chopped
1 lg. clove of garlic, minced
Salt and pepper to taste
1 No. 2 can spinach
½ c. chopped parsley
1 can sliced mushrooms
2 cans tomato sauce
1 tsp. each oregano, sage, rosemary
1 c. grated cheese
1 lb. shell macaroni, cooked

Saute ground beef with onions, garlic, salt and pepper in skillet until crumbly. Combine spinach, parsley, mushrooms, tomato sauce and herbs in saucepan. Simmer for 1 hour. Alternate layers of ground beef mixture, macaroni, and spinach mixture in greased casserole until all ingredients are used. Top with cheese. Bake at 350 degrees for 20 minutes. Yield: 6-8 servings.

Marlene Figone
Manteca, California

Spanish Macaroni

1 med. onion, chopped
½ green pepper, chopped
1 tbsp. margarine
¼ to ½ lb. ground beef
½ tsp. salt
Pepper to taste
1 10½-oz. can tomato soup
¼ lb. cheese, cubed
1 c. macaroni, cooked
Bread crumbs

Saute onion and green pepper in margarine in skillet until tender. Add next 3 ingredients. Cook, stirring, until ground beef is brown and crumbly. Add soup, cheese and macaroni; mix well. Place in baking dish. Top with bread crumbs. Bake at 350 degrees for 25 to 30 minutes. Yield: 4 servings.

Margaret K. Gorman
Ansonia, Connecticut

Hamburger Meal-In-One

1 lb. hamburger
1 med. onion, chopped
1 7-oz. box macaroni
2 cans tomato soup
¾ c. catsup
1 tbsp. Worcestershire sauce
1 tsp. salt
¼ tsp. pepper
½ lb. American cheese, grated
1 c. finely crushed potato chips

Saute hamburger with onion in skillet until crumbly. Add remaining ingredients except potato chips; mix well. Pour into greased casserole. Bake at 350 degrees for 45 minutes. Top with potato chips. Bake for 15 minutes longer. Yield: 6 servings.

Loretta Schrowang
Hennepin, Illinois

Aunt Jone's Lasagna

1 clove of garlic, minced
1 onion, chopped
2 tbsp. oil
1½ lb. ground beef
24 oz. tomato paste
2 tsp. salt
¼ tsp. pepper
1 tsp. basil
Italian seasoning to taste
1 tsp. oregano
½ lb. lasagna noodles, cooked
16 to 24-oz. mozzarella cheese, shredded

Saute garlic and onion in oil in skillet until tender. Add ground beef stirring until crumbly. Add tomato paste, seasonings and 3 cups hot water; blend well. Simmer for 30 minutes. Alternate layers of sauce, noodles and cheese in large baking dish until all ingredients are used, ending with cheese. Bake at 350 degrees for 30 minutes. Let stand for 15 minutes before serving. Yield: 6-8 servings.

Penny Hammer
Sterling, Illinois

Cashew-Beef Bake

1 lb. ground chuck
1 c. chopped onions
1 c. diced celery
1 8-oz. package noodles, cooked, drained
1 can cream of chicken soup
1 can cream of mushroom soup
1 c. milk
1 tsp. salt
¼ tsp. pepper
1 c. salted cashews

Saute ground beef in skillet until crumbly. Add onions and celery; cook until tender. Layer noodles and ground beef mixture in greased 2-quart casserole. Combine remaining ingredients except cashews in bowl; mix well. Pour into casserole. Bake, covered, at 325 degrees for 1 hour. Uncover; sprinkle with cashews. Bake for 10 minutes longer. Yield: 8 servings.

Mary Kaye Hancock
Sesser, Illinois

Fried Noodle Casserole

1 lg. can chow mein noodles
1 can mushrooms
1 lb. ground beef
1 onion, minced
½ c. celery
2 cans cream of chicken soup

Combine all ingredients except soup in bowl; mix well. Place in casserole. Combine soup with 1 soup can water in bowl; mix well. Pour over casserole. Bake at 350 degrees for 45 minutes. Yield: 4 servings.

Mardelle Shager
Glencoe, Minnesota

Hamburger-Cheese Bake

1 lb. ground beef
½ c. chopped onion
2 8-oz. cans tomato sauce
1 tsp. sugar
¾ tsp. salt
¼ tsp. garlic salt
¼ tsp. pepper
4 c. medium noodles
1 c. cottage cheese
1 8-oz. package cream cheese, softened
¼ c. sour cream
⅓ c. sliced green onion
¼ c. chopped green pepper
¼ c. shredded Parmesan cheese

Brown ground beef and chopped onion in skillet; stir in next 5 ingredients. Cook noodles using package directions; drain. Combine remaining ingredients except Parmesan cheese; mix well. Layer half the noodles, half the ground beef mixture and all the cottage cheese mixture in 11 × 7-inch baking dish. Add remaining noodles and ground beef mixture. Top with Parmesan cheese. Bake at 350 degrees for ½ hour. Yield: 8-10 servings.

Mrs. Ivell Halseide
Culbertson, Montana

Hamburger-Corn Casserole

1 lb. ground beef
1 onion, chopped
1 green pepper, chopped
1 pkg. frozen corn, thawed
Salt and pepper to taste
6 oz. fine egg noodles
1 lg. can tomato juice
Grated American cheese

Saute ground beef with onion and green pepper in skillet until crumbly. Stir in corn, salt and pepper. Layer uncooked noodles and ground beef mixture in buttered 1½-quart casserole, ending with ground beef layer. Add tomato juice; top with cheese. Bake at 350 degrees for ½ hour or until noodles are cooked and cheese melted. Yield: 6 servings.

Ruth R. Harberleu
Greensburg, Pennsylvania

Ned's Goop

1½ lb. ground chuck
Salt and pepper
1 tbsp. chili powder
Dash of monosodium glutamate
1 lg. onion, chopped
1 green pepper, chopped
1 sm. can chopped mushrooms
1 c. grated cheese
1 sm. bottle sliced olives
1 No. 303 can whole kernel corn
1 pkg. small noodles, cooked, drained
2 cans cream of tomato soup
Toasted almonds

Saute ground beef with seasonings, onion, green pepper and mushrooms until crumbly. Add next 5 ingredients; mix well. Pour into casserole. Bake at 350 degrees for ½ hour or until bubbly. Top with almonds.

Janiece Crisp Byrd
Banquete, Texas

Helen's Beef-Noodle Bake

1 lb. ground beef
1 lg. onion, sliced
1 tsp. salt
¼ tsp. pepper
1 can tomato soup
1 sm. can sliced mushrooms, drained
½ lb. process American cheese, diced
1 pkg. wide noodles, cooked, drained

Saute ground beef with onion in skillet until crumbly. Add remaining ingredients except noodles. Cook over low heat until cheese melts. Stir in noodles. Place in 2-quart casserole. Bake at 350 degrees until lightly browned.

Helen Roberts
Alvin, Texas

Surprise Casserole

1 lb. hamburger
Salt and pepper to taste
¾ c. cubed cheese
1 pkg. egg noodles
1 can cream of mushroom soup
1 can cream of celery soup
2 tbsp. grated Parmesan cheese
½ c. bread crumbs

Season hamburger with salt and pepper. Shape into bite-sized meatballs around cubes of cheese. Saute meatballs in skillet until brown on all sides; drain. Cook noodles using package directions. Place in lightly greased casserole. Stir in soups, Parmesan cheese and meatballs. Top with bread crumbs. Bake in 375-degree oven for 45 minutes. Yield: 4-6 servings.

Cathy DiOrio
Burbank, Illinois

Pizza Casserole

½ to 1 lb. ground beef
1 can pizza sauce
1 c. milk
1 sm. can mushrooms
1 c. grated mozzarella cheese
1 c. wide noodles
1½ tsp. oregano
½ to 1 tsp. garlic salt

Saute ground beef in skillet until crumbly. Combine with remaining ingredients in baking dish; mix well. Refrigerate for 4 hours or longer. Bake at 350 degrees for 1 hour.

Donna Pomerenke
Walnut Grove, Minnesota

Beef and Rice Casserole

1 lb. ground beef
½ c. chopped onion
1 c. chopped celery
¼ c. chopped green pepper
1 c. uncooked rice
1 lg. can tomatoes
1 tsp. salt
1 tbsp. chili powder
¼ tsp. pepper
½ tsp. Worcestershire sauce
1 c. chopped ripe olives

Saute ground beef with next 4 ingredients in skillet until crumbly. Add remaining ingredients. Bring to a boil. Pour into 2-quart casserole. Bake, covered, at 325 degrees for 1 hour. Yield: 6-8 servings.

Marjorie W. Browning
Pensacola, Florida

Casserole Italiano

1½ lb. zucchini, sliced ¼ inch thick
1 c. minced onion
1 sm. clove of garlic, minced
2 tbsp. butter
1 lb. ground beef
1 c. minute rice
1 tsp. basil
2 c. creamed cottage cheese
1 can condensed tomato soup
1 c. shredded sharp American cheese

Cook zucchini in a small amount of boiling salted water in saucepan until tender-crisp; drain. Saute onion and garlic in butter in heavy skillet until onion is transparent. Add ground beef. Cook until lightly browned, stirring occasionally. Stir in rice and basil. Arrange half the zucchini in bottom of buttered 2½-quart casserole. Top with ground beef. Spread with cottage cheese. Arrange remaining zucchini over top. Combine soup with ⅔ cup water. Pour over zucchini. Sprinkle with cheese. Bake at 350 degrees for 35 to 40 minutes until lightly browned. Yield: 6-8 servings.

Picture for this recipe on page 25.

Mock Chow Mein

1 lb. hamburger
1 onion, chopped
1 can cream of mushroom soup
1½ c. diced celery
½ c. rice
4 tbsp. soy sauce
1 can mushroom pieces (opt.)

Saute hamburger with onion in skillet until crumbly; drain. Add remaining ingredients with 2 soup cans water; mix well. Place in greased casserole. Bake at 350 degrees for 1½ hours, stirring often. Yield: 8 servings.

Kathleen Berg
Jerome, Arizona

Seven-Layer Casserole

1 c. rice
1 c. canned whole kernel corn
Salt and pepper to taste
2 cans tomato sauce
¾ lb. ground beef
½ c. finely chopped onion
¼ c. finely chopped green pepper
4 slices bacon, cut into halves

Combine rice and corn with seasoning in casserole. Mix 1 can tomato sauce with 1 sauce can water in bowl; pour over casserole. Combine ground beef, onion and green pepper in bowl; mix well. Add to casserole. Mix 1 can tomato sauce and ½ can water in bowl; add to casserole. Arrange bacon on top. Bake, covered, at 350 degrees for 1 hour. Uncover. Bake ½ hour longer or until bacon is crisp. Yield: 6 servings.

Myra D. Sorensen
Ritchfield, Utah

Cuban Spaghetti

2 lb. hamburger
3 lg. onions, chopped
1 lg. green pepper, chopped
½ lg. bunch celery, chopped
2 cans tomato soup
Red pepper
Black pepper
Salt
Tabasco sauce
1 can mushrooms, drained
1 can peas, drained
1 pkg. spaghetti, partially cooked
1 lb. sharp cheese, grated
1 bottle stuffed olives

Saute hamburger with onions in skillet until crumbly. Add next 3 ingredients and season to taste. Alternate layers of sauce with remaining ingredients in baking dish until all ingredients are used. Bake at 325 degrees for 1 hour. Yield: 12 servings.

Sara Gantt
Wagener, South Carolina

Elaine's Spaghetti Casserole

1 lb. hamburger
1 tsp. salt
½ tsp. pepper
¼ c. chopped green pepper
2 c. spaghetti, cooked, drained
1 can tomato sauce
1 can tomato soup
½ c. cheese cubes

Brown hamburger in skillet stirring until crumbly. Combine with remaining ingredients except cheese in casserole; mix well. Top with cheese. Bake at 350 degrees for 45 minutes to 1 hour. Yield: 6 servings.

Elaine Peters
Mohall, North Dakota

Mexican Spaghetti

1 lb. ground beef
1 lb. pork sausage
1 c. chopped onions
½ c. chopped green pepper
1 tsp. each salt, pepper
2 tbsp. cayenne pepper
2 c. canned tomatoes
2 8-oz. cans tomato sauce
1 8-oz. package spaghetti, cooked
1 c. grated Cheddar cheese

Brown first 4 ingredients in heavy skillet, stirring until crumbly. Drain. Add remaining ingredients except cheese with ½ cup water; mix well. Simmer for 10 minutes. Pour into 2-quart buttered casserole. Bake for 20 minutes at 400 degrees. Top with grated cheese. Bake for 10 minutes longer. Yield: 6-8 servings.

Linda Clark
Channelview, Texas

Spaghetti-Almond Casserole

1½ lb. lean ground beef
2 tbsp. olive oil
2 lg. onions, sliced
1 green pepper, diced
1 clove of garlic, minced
2 8-oz. cans tomato sauce
1 4-oz. can mushrooms, drained
Salt and pepper to taste
2 bay leaves
1 tbsp. Worcestershire sauce
1 7-oz. package spaghetti, cooked
2 c. grated sharp cheese
2 c. slivered almonds

Saute ground beef in olive oil in skillet until crumbly; drain. Add next 3 ingredients. Cook until onions are soft. Stir in tomato sauce, mushrooms and seasonings. Simmer for 30 minutes, stirring frequently and adding water if necessary. Remove bay leaves and add spaghetti; mix well. Spoon into two 1½-quart casseroles. Sprinkle with cheese and almonds. Bake at 350 degrees for 30 minutes. Yield: 8-10 servings.

Kay Ryan
Pontiac, Michigan

Vegetable-Spaghetti Casserole

1 lb. ground beef
1 sm. onion, chopped
Salt
Pepper
Paprika
1 can tomato soup
1 No. 2 can mixed vegetables
1 c. spaghetti, cooked
½ c. grated cheese

Brown ground beef with onion and seasonings in skillet, stirring until crumbly. Add remaining ingredients, except cheese with ½ cup water; mix well. Pour into greased casserole. Bake at 350 degrees for 20 to 25 minutes. Top with cheese. Bake until cheese melts.

Elizabeth Richardson
Orangeburg, South Carolina

Chalupas

1 lb. ground beef
1 c. chopped onion
2 tbsp. melted butter
2 tbsp. flour
3 tbsp. chili powder
1½ c. tomato soup
1½ c. light cream
Salt to taste
12 tortillas, cut in strips
1½ c. grated American cheese

Saute ground beef with ½ cup onion in butter in skillet until crumbly. Stir in flour and chili powder. Cook for 5 minutes. Add 1 cup water; blend well. Simmer, covered, until thick. Combine soup, cream, salt and remaining onion in bowl; blend well. Alternate layers of tortilla strips, ground beef mixture, soup mixture and cheese in greased casserole until all ingredients are used. Bake at 325 degrees until browned and bubbly. Yield: 6 servings.

Mabel Moorhouse
Belen, New Mexico

Chili Pot

2 bunches green onions, chopped
1 clove of garlic
1 lb. ground beef
Salt and pepper to taste
2 c. cooked pinto beans
1 can enchilada sauce
1 c. grated cheese
Corn chips

Saute onions and garlic in skillet until tender. Add ground beef and seasonings. Cook, stirring until crumbly. Stir in beans and sauce. Simmer for 10 minutes. Alternate layers of ground beef mixture, cheese and corn chips in casserole until all ingredients are used. Bake at 350 degrees for 20 minutes. Yield: 6-8 servings.

Betty Hall
Fort Cobb, Oklahoma

Belmont Mexi-Chili Casserole

1 lb. ground beef
1 1-lb. can kidney beans, rinsed, drained
1 15-oz. can enchilada sauce
1 8-oz. can tomato sauce
1 tbsp. instant minced onion
1 c. corn chips
2 c. shredded Cheddar cheese
1½ c. sour cream

Brown ground beef in skillet, stirring until crumbly. Add next 5 ingredients and 1½ cups cheese; mix well. Pour into 2-quart casserole. Bake at 375 degrees for 20 to 25 minutes until bubbly. Spread with sour cream and remaining cheese. Bake 3 to 4 minutes longer until cheese melts. Yield: 6 servings.

Carol Hepburn
Belmont, California

Creamed Tacos

1½ lb. ground beef
1 lg. onion, diced
1 lg. green pepper, diced
Salt and pepper to taste
1 6-oz. can hot sauce
1 6-oz. can enchilada sauce
1 pkg. tortillas
½ lb. cheese, grated
1 lg. can evaporated milk

Saute ground beef in skillet until crumbly. Add onion, green pepper and seasonings. Cook until tender. Stir in sauces. Alternate layers of tortillas, sauce and cheese in greased casserole. Pour milk over casserole. Bake at 350 degrees for 45 minutes. Yield: 8 servings.

Rachel Pearce
Fort Worth, Texas

Enchilada Casserole

1 10-oz. can Mexican-style tomato sauce
1 8-oz. can tomato sauce
1 lb. ground beef
1 lg. onion, chopped
2 cloves of garlic, chopped
1 hard-boiled egg, chopped (opt.)
1 4½-oz. can chopped ripe olives
½ tsp. salt
6 tortillas
½ lb. Monterey Jack cheese, grated

Combine first 2 ingredients with 1¼ cups water in saucepan; warm over low heat. Brown ground beef, onion and garlic in skillet, stirring until crumbly. Add egg, olives, salt and ½ cup tomato mixture; mix well. Dip tortillas in tomato mixture; layer in casserole with meat mixture and cheese. Top with remaining sauce and cheese. Bake at 350 degrees for 25 minutes. Yield: 6 servings.

Maxine Barber
Martinez, California

Party Polenta

3 lb. ground beef
2 onions, chopped
1 1-lb. 13-oz. can tomatoes
1 6-oz. can tomato paste
4 tsp. chili powder
2 tsp. salt
½ tsp. hot sauce
1 12-oz. package corn muffin mix
¼ c. grated Parmesan cheese

Saute beef with onions in deep saucepan, stirring occasionally, until brown. Drain. Add tomatoes, tomato paste, chili powder, salt and hot sauce; mix well. Pour into 3-quart casserole. Prepare corn muffin mix using package directions. Spread over top of casserole. Sprinkle with cheese. Bake at 400 degrees for 35 to 40 minutes or until crust is brown. Yield: 12 servings.

Winnie Steel
Des Moines, Iowa

Spanish Pronto Loaf

1 lb. ground beef
1 med. onion, diced
1 c. grated Cheddar cheese
1 c. tostados

2 sm. jalapeno peppers, thinly sliced
½ tsp. garlic powder
1 tsp. salt
½ tsp. pepper
¼ c. evaporated milk

Brown ground beef and onion in skillet, stirring until crumbly. Alternate layers of cheese, tostados, ground beef, jalapenos and seasonings in 5 × 8-inch casserole. Pour milk over top. Bake at 375 degrees for 30 minutes.

Betty Sadberry
Amherst, Texas

Taco Pie

1 lb. ground beef
1 bottle taco sauce
2 c. corn chips
1 c. grated Cheddar cheese

Saute ground beef in skillet until crumbly. Add taco sauce. Simmer for 15 minutes. Layer corn chips, ground beef and cheese in baking dish. Bake at 350 degrees for 10 minutes or until cheese melts. Yield: 2-4 servings.

Sylvia Smith
Stanfield, Oregon

Tamale Bake

1 lb. ground beef
½ c. diced onion
¼ c. diced green pepper
½ c. diced celery
½ c. corn meal
1 No. 2 can tomatoes
1 No. 2 can whole kernel corn
½ c. chopped olives
2½ tsp. salt
1½ tsp. chili powder
1½ tsp. Worcestershire sauce
½ c. grated American-cheese

Saute ground beef with onion, green pepper and celery in skillet until crumbly. Combine cornmeal and tomatoes in saucepan. Cook for 5 to 10 minutes, stirring constantly. Add to ground beef mixture with remaining ingredients except cheese; mix well. Pour into greased casserole. Top with cheese. Bake at 325 degrees for 45 minutes.

Katherine Elrod
Lubbock, Texas

Elodee's Tamale Pie

1 c. chopped onions
1 c. chopped green peppers
¾ lb. ground beef
2 8-oz. cans seasoned tomato sauce
1 12-oz. can whole kernel corn, drained
1 c. chopped ripe olives
1 clove of garlic, minced
1 tbsp. sugar
2 to 3 tsp. chili powder
Dash of pepper
Salt
1½ c. shredded sharp process American
   cheese
¾ c. yellow cornmeal
1 tbsp. butter

Saute onion and green pepper in skillet until tender. Add ground beef. Brown lightly, stirring until crumbly. Add next 7 ingredients with 1 teaspoon salt; mix well. Simmer for 20 to 25 minutes. Add cheese; stir until melted. Spoon into greased 6 × 10-inch baking dish. Combine cornmeal and ½ teaspoon salt with 2 cups cold water in saucepan. Cook until thick, stirring constantly. Stir in butter. Spoon meat mixture in 3 lengthwise strips. Bake at 375 degrees for 40 minutes. Yield: 6 servings.

Elodee McCormick
Dade City, Florida

Easy Tamale Pie

Cornmeal
1 tsp. salt
Seasoning to taste
1½ lb. ground beef
1 lg. onion, diced
1 can pitted olives
2 c. tomatoes, cooked
1 No. 2 can cream-style corn

Combine 1 cup cornmeal with 4 cups water, salt and seasoning in saucepan. Cook until thick, stirring constantly. Brown ground beef and onion in skillet, stirring until crumbly. Stir in remaining ingredients with a small amount of cornmeal. Cook until thickened, stirring frequently. Line greased 9 × 12-inch baking dish with cornmeal mixture. Spoon ground beef mixture over top. Bake, covered, at 350 degrees for 30 minutes. Yield: 8 servings.

Margaret Wahl
Stockton, California

Polynesian Meat Rolls

1½ lb. ground round
1 egg
½ c. rice
½ c. soft bread crumbs
½ c. milk
½ c. chopped onions
1 clove of garlic, crushed
1 tsp. salt
¼ tsp. pepper
1 tbsp. soy sauce
1 pt. broth
1 6-oz. can sweet and sour sauce

Combine first 10 ingredients in bowl; mix well. Shape into serving-sized rolls. Arrange in single layer in shallow casserole. Pour broth over rolls. Bake, covered, at 350 degrees for 1½ hours. Spoon sauce over each roll. Bake, uncovered, for 15 to 20 minutes longer.

Janice K. Fruland
Ontario, Canada

Stuffed Beef Bake

1½ lb. lean ground beef
1 egg
¼ c. minced onion
1 tsp. salt
¼ tsp. pepper
1 8-oz. can tomato sauce
2 c. soft bread cubes
2 tbsp. minced onion
1 tbsp. pickle relish
1 tsp. mustard
¼ tsp. seasoned salt

Combine first 5 ingredients with ¼ cup tomato sauce in bowl; mix well. Pack into shallow 6 × 10-inch baking dish. Make 6 wells on top of ground beef mixture. Mix remaining ingredients; fill wells. Bake for 30 minutes at 350 degrees; drain off drippings. Bake for 20 minutes longer. Yield: 6 servings.

Sister Patrick Marie
Mendhorn, New Jersey

Best Hot Dish

1½ to 2 lb. ground round
1 onion, diced
2 c. diced celery
2 cans cream of mushroom soup
1 can cream

1 can mixed vegetables
1 can mushrooms
4 tbsp. soy sauce
2 lg. cans chow mein noodles

Saute ground round with onion in large skillet until crumbly. Add remaining ingredients, reserving a few chow mein noodles; mix well. Place in casserole; top with reserved noodles. Bake at 325 degrees for 1 hour. Yield: 6 servings.

Betty Lund
Nashwauk, Minnesota

Beef Patty Casserole

2 lb. ground beef
Freshly ground pepper
1 c. soft bread crumbs
½ c. tomato juice
1 egg
½ tsp. curry powder
2 lg. onions, thinly sliced
2 lb. potatoes, peeled, thinly sliced
3 c. beef broth

Combine first 6 ingredients in bowl; mix well. Form into patties about ¼-inch thick. Saute patties in skillet until brown. Remove patties; brown onions in skillet. Alternate layers of potatoes, onions and beef patties in 3-quart casserole, ending with potatoes. Cover with beef broth. Bake at 350 degrees for 45 minutes or until brown. Yield: 6-8 servings.

Mrs. Evelyn Fuller
Selma, Alabama

Cauliflower-Beef Casserole

1 med. head cauliflower
1½ lb. ground beef
1 sm. onion, chopped
½ tsp. salt
½ tsp. Tabasco sauce
1 tbsp. flour
1 c. milk
1 tbsp. oil
½ lb. cheese, grated
1 c. seasoned bread cubes

Separate cauliflower buds. Cook in salted water in saucepan until tender-crisp. Saute ground beef with onion, salt and ¼ teaspoon Tabasco in skillet. Blend flour, milk, oil and ¼ teaspoon Tabasco in small saucepan. Cook

over low heat until thickened, stirring constantly. Add cheese. Heat until melted. Place ground beef mixture in 2-quart casserole. Cover with bread cubes; add cauliflower. Top with cheese sauce. Bake at 375 degrees for 30 minutes or until bubbly. Yield: 6 servings.

Picture for this recipe on page 19.

Cheeseburger Casserole

1 lb. ground beef
1 med. onion, shredded
1 tsp. salt
⅛ tsp. pepper
1 tbsp. Worcestershire sauce
1 12-oz. can whole kernel corn, drained
1 c. shredded cheese
¾ c. catsup
½ c. potato chip crumbs

Saute ground beef with onion in skillet until crumbly. Add remaining ingredients except crumbs; mix well. Place in casserole; top with crumbs. Bake at 350 degrees for ½ hour. Yield: 5-6 servings.

Mrs. George Wooton
Nebo, Kentucky

Barbecued Meatballs and Beans

1 lb. ground beef
1 egg, beaten
½ c. fine dry bread crumbs
⅔ c. milk
1 tsp. salt
⅛ tsp. pepper
1 16 or 18-oz. can pork and beans
½ c. catsup
2 tbsp. brown sugar
2 tbsp. vinegar
1 tbsp. Worcestershire sauce
¾ c. chopped onions

Combine first 6 ingredients in bowl; mix well. Shape into balls. Saute in skillet until brown on all sides. Layer half the beans in 1½-quart casserole; top with meatballs. Add remaining beans. Combine remaining ingredients in bowl; mix well. Pour into casserole. Bake, covered, at 350 degrees for 20 minutes. Uncover. Bake for 20 minutes longer. Yield: 6 servings.

Mrs. Richard Kunz
Ellsworth A. F. B., South Dakota

Beef and Green Bean Casserole

1 lb. ground beef
1 can French-style green beans, drained
1 sm. can sliced mushrooms, drained
1 sm. package slivered almonds
1 can cream of celery soup
1 can cream of mushroom soup
1 sm. package Tater Tots

Saute ground beef in skillet until lightly browned; drain. Toss ground beef with green beans, mushrooms and almonds in bowl. Combine soups with 1 soup can hot water in bowl; mix well. Pour over green bean mixture; toss lightly. Spoon into casserole. Arrange Tater Tots over top. Bake at 350 degrees for 25 minutes or until brown.

Mrs. Brett W. Slusser
Agra, Oklahoma

Three-Bean Burger Bake

½ lb. bacon
1½ to 2 lb. hamburger
1 c. chopped onion
¾ c. packed brown sugar
½ c. catsup
1 tsp. vinegar
1 tsp. mustard
⅛ tsp. salt
2 c. pork and beans
2 c. drained lima beans
2 c. drained kidney beans

Cut bacon into 1-inch pieces. Saute hamburger with bacon and onion in skillet until crumbly; drain. Combine with remaining ingredients in bowl; mix well. Place in 2½-quart casserole. Bake at 325 degrees for 1 hour.

Kathy Steckel
Merrill, Wisconsin

Beef-Tomato-Cabbage Scallop

1 lb. ground beef
¼ c. chopped onion
1 c. chopped celery
2½ c. chopped tomatoes
2 tsp. salt
1 tsp. pepper
4 c. chopped cabbage
1 c. soft bread crumbs

Saute beef in skillet with onion and celery until crumbly. Add tomatoes, salt and pepper. Bring to boiling point. Alternate layers of cabbage and ground beef mixture in buttered 2-quart baking dish. Top with bread crumbs. Bake in 375-degree oven for 40 minutes or until bubbly. Yield: 6 servings.

Mrs. Virginia Collie
Dry Fork, Virginia

Harvest Special

1 lb. ground beef
1 med. onion, chopped
2 green peppers, sliced
1½ tsp. salt
¼ tsp. pepper
½ tsp. thyme
2 c. fresh-cut corn
4 tomatoes, sliced
½ c. soft bread crumbs

Saute ground beef with onion and peppers in skillet until crumbly. Add seasonings. Layer half the corn, ground beef mixture and tomatoes in 2-quart casserole. Repeat layers; cover with bread crumbs. Bake at 350 degrees for 35 minutes. Yield: 4 servings.

Mrs. Inez F. Klein
Malverne, New York

Main Dish Zucchini Lasagna

½ lb. ground beef
⅓ c. chopped onion
1 15-oz. can tomato sauce
½ tsp. salt
½ tsp. oregano
¼ tsp. basil
⅛ tsp. pepper
4 med. zucchini
1 8-oz. carton cottage cheese
1 egg
2 tbsp. flour
¼ lb. mozzarella cheese, shredded

Brown ground beef with onion in skillet until crumbly; drain well. Add next 5 ingredients. Simmer for 5 minutes. Slice zucchini, lengthwise ¼ inch thick. Blend cottage cheese and egg in bowl. Alternate layers of zucchini; flour, cottage cheese mixture and sauce until all ingredients are used. Top with mozzarella cheese. Bake at 375 degrees for 40 minutes. Let stand for 10 minutes before cutting.

Jeanette Moncel
Francesville, Indiana

Pork

Apple-Pork Chop Casserole

4 to 6 pork loin chops
1 No. 2½ can sauerkraut
2 tbsp. brown sugar
1 med. apple, chopped

Fry pork chops in skillet until well done. Place chops in casserole. Spread sauerkraut and liquid over chops. Sprinkle with brown sugar and apple. Bake, covered, at 350 degrees for 1½ hours. Add ¼ cup water during baking if necessary. Yield: 4-6 servings.

Beverly Bayer
North Plainfield, New Jersey

Baked Pork Chops Normande

4 to 6 pork loin chops
Dash of salt and pepper
3 lg. apples, thinly sliced
2 tsp. sugar
2 tsp. cinnamon
1 tbsp. butter
1 lg. bay leaf
2 tbsp. onion, grated
3 whole cloves
½ c. cider

Season chops with salt and pepper. Arrange in buttered baking dish. Cover with apples. Sprinkle with sugar and cinnamon. Dot with butter. Bake, covered, at 400 degrees for 1½ hours. Remove cover. Bake for 15 minutes longer. Yield: 4-6 servings.

Jane Ann Sloan
Covina, California

Baked Pork Roll-Ups

12 to 14 slices thin pork steaks
Salt and pepper
Prepared mustard
4 c. soft bread crumbs
½ c. raisins
½ c. chopped celery
½ c. chopped apple
1 tsp. salt
2 tsp. sage
Flour

Trim steaks and remove bone. Saute lightly in skillet to render fat. Pound to ¼-inch thickness; season. Spread lightly with mustard. Combine crumbs, raisins, celery, apple, salt and sage in bowl. Spread on steaks. Roll up and fasten with toothpicks. Dust with flour. Brown in small amount of shortening in skillet. Place in 3-quart casserole. Add 1 cup hot water. Bake, covered, at 350 degrees for 1 hour. Yield: 12 servings.

Mrs. Mann Nutt
Hohenwald, Tennessee

Bernice's Pork Chop Casserole

Salt and pepper
6 pork chops
1 med. onion, sliced
Sliced fresh tomato (opt.)
1 c. rice
1 can beef consomme

Salt and pepper pork chops. Place in casserole. Lay a slice of onion and tomato on each chop. Cover with rice. Add consomme and 1 soup can water. Bake at 350 degrees for 1 hour or until tender. Yield: 6 servings.

Bernice Britt
Saratoga, Texas

Chop-Top Casserole

1½ c. dried white beans
1 lg. onion
1 med. bay leaf
1½ tsp. salt
4 thick lean pork chops
Garlic salt
Coarsely ground black pepper
1 1-lb can stewed tomatoes

Cook beans using package directions, adding whole onion and bay leaf. Stir in salt when beans are nearly tender. Cook until tender. Remove onion and bay leaf. Drain beans slightly. Brown pork chops, sprinkling generously with garlic salt and pepper. Remove chops from skillet. Add tomatoes, stirring to blend in meat juices. Add beans. Pour into 2-quart casserole. Arrange chops on top. Bake at 350 degrees for 1 hour or until chops are fork tender. Yield: 4 servings.

Jean S. McHargue
Beltsville, Maryland

Fruited Pork Chop Casserole

4 pork chops
1 onion, sliced
1½ c. dried prunes
2 tbsp. lemon juice
½ tsp. dried mustard
½ tsp. Worcestershire sauce
3 whole cloves
1 tsp. salt
Paprika

Brown chops in skillet. Place in casserole. Cover with onion. Arrange prunes around chops. Combine lemon juice, mustard, Worcestershire sauce, cloves, salt and ¾ cup hot water in bowl. Pour over chops. Sprinkle with paprika. Bake, covered, at 325 degrees for 1 hour.

Muriel W. Corliss
St. Johnsbury, Vermont

Hidden Treasure

6 lean pork chops
Salt and pepper
2 c. chopped onions
1 c. rice
1 can tomatoes
½ c. sugar

Lay chops in baking dish. Sprinkle with salt, pepper and 1 cup onion. Spread rice over chops. Cover with tomatoes, remaining onion, sugar and salt and pepper to taste. Bake, covered, at 350 degrees for 1½ hours. Yield: 6 servings.

Sally Cheney
Wenatchee, Washington

Nancy's Pork Chop Casserole

4 lg. pork chops
4 c. soft bread crumbs
¼ tsp. pepper
4 tbsp. each chopped onion, green
   pepper
2 tbsp. chopped parsley
Salt
1 apple, quartered

Brown pork chops in skillet over low heat. Remove chops. Stir bread crumbs into pan drippings. Add pepper, vegetables and ½ teaspoon salt. Place in baking dish. Arrange pork chops over dressing. Top with apple. Sprinkle with salt. Bake at 350 degrees for 1 hour. Yield: 4 servings.

Nancy Willard
East Haven, Connecticut

One-Dish Pork Chop Dinner

6 pork chops
4 c. cooked noodles
Salt to taste
½ tsp. pepper
1 tbsp. Worcestershire sauce
½ tsp. monosodium glutamate
2 tbsp. grated onion
1 can condensed tomato soup

Brown chops in skillet. Place noodles in greased casserole. Combine remaining ingredients with ½ cup water in bowl; mix well. Pour over noodles. Place chops around edge of casserole. Bake, covered, at 350 degrees for 1 hour. Yield: 4-6 servings.

Mattie Finney
Burton, Washington

Pork Chops with Apricot Dressing

8 pork chops
½ c. rice
¼ c. minced onion
⅓ lb. dried apricots, chopped
5 tsp. dried parsley
¼ tsp. salt
Dash of pepper
⅓ c. sugar
1 tsp. grated lemon rind
2⅔ c. chicken broth

Brown chops in skillet. Set aside. Saute rice and onions in pan drippings until brown. Add next 6 ingredients; mix well. Alternate layers of pork chops and rice mixture in large casserole ending with rice mixture. Pour chicken broth over all. Bake at 350 degrees for 1 hour or until liquid is absorbed. Yield: 8 servings.

Mrs. Edgar Barber
Wall, South Dakota

Pork and Brown Rice Casserole

1½ c. brown rice
2 tsp. salt
½ to 1 c. chopped almonds
1 c. chopped celery
6 pork chops
¼ tsp. pepper

Cook rice in 3 cups boiling water with 1½ teaspoons salt until tender. Add nuts and celery. Place mixture in 9 × 13 × 2-inch baking pan. Arrange chops on top. Season chops with remaining salt and pepper. Bake at 350 degrees for 1 hour. Yield: 6 servings.

Laura Anderson
Sutherlin, Oregon

Pork Chops with Curry Stuffing

1¼ c. chopped apple
⅓ c. diced onion
½ c. chopped celery
6 slices whole wheat bread, crumbled
⅓ c. milk
¾ tsp. curry powder
½ tsp. salt
6 1-inch pork chops with pockets
¼ c. flour
¼ tsp. pepper
2 tbsp. shortening

Saute first 3 ingredients in skillet until golden. Combine bread crumbs and milk in bowl. Stir in apple mixture, ½ teaspoon curry powder and ¼ teaspoon salt. Stuff pork chops with stuffing. Combine flour, pepper, ¼ teaspoon curry powder and ¼ teaspoon salt. Coat chops with flour; brown in shortening in skillet. Place in 3-quart casserole. Bake, covered, at 350 degrees for 1 hour.

Shelba Barnes
Rossville, Indiana

Pork Chops Florentine

6 loin pork chops
Seasoned salt
2 pkg. frozen spinach
3 tbsp. margarine
3 tbsp. flour
1 c. milk
1 tsp. salt

⅛ tsp. pepper
½ c. grated Cheddar cheese
Bottled mustard sauce

Trim fat from chops. Brown in skillet until golden. Sprinkle with seasoned salt. Cook spinach using package directions; drain. Melt margarine in skillet. Add flour, stirring to make smooth paste. Add next 4 ingredients. Cook until smooth, stirring constantly. Add spinach; mix well. Place in 1-quart greased casserole. Arrange chops on top. Bake, covered, at 350 degrees for 30 minutes. Remove cover. Bake for 15 minutes longer or until chops are tender. Serve with mustard sauce. Yield: 6 servings.

Alma R. Frerichs
Grants Pass, Oregon

Pork Chop-Potato Bake

5 med. potatoes, peeled
Salt and pepper to taste
1 tbsp. instant minced onion
6 pork chops
1 to 2 cans cream of mushroom soup

Slice potatoes ¼ inch thick. Place in large buttered casserole. Sprinkle with salt, pepper and onion. Brown pork chops in skillet. Place over potatoes. Spread soup over chops. Pour 1 soup can water over soup. Cover. Bake at 350 degrees for 1 to 2 hours. Yield: 6 servings.

Margaret Raburn
Marlow, Oklahoma

Pork Chop-Potato Scallop

4 pork chops
1 can cream of mushroom soup
½ c. sour cream
4 c. thinly sliced potatoes
2 tbsp. chopped parsley
1 med. onion, sliced (opt.)
1 tsp. salt
¼ tsp. pepper

Brown pork chops in skillet. Combine soup, sour cream and ¼ cup water in bowl; mix well. Layer potatoes, parsley, onion, soup mixture and chops in 2-quart casserole. Sprinkle with salt and pepper. Bake, covered, at 375 degrees for 1¼ hours. Yield: 4 servings.

Bernadine Herring
Bayard, New Mexico

Pork Chops on Scalloped Potatoes

Potatoes, peeled, sliced
¼ c. margarine
4 tbsp. flour
¼ c. chopped Velveeta cheese
Salt and pepper to taste
2 c. milk
Pork chops

Arrange alternate layers of potatoes, margarine, flour, cheese, salt and pepper in 2-quart casserole. Pour milk over layers. Arrange pork chops on top of potatoes. Bake at 350 degrees for 1½ hours.

Jane Davis
Corpus Christi, Texas

Pork Chops with Waldorf Rice

4 ¾-in. lean pork chops, trimmed
Salt and pepper
¾ c. rice
1 c. cubed apple
1 c. diced celery
¼ c. minced onion

Season chops with salt and pepper. Brown in skillet. Place chops in casserole. Dissolve ½ teaspoon salt in 2 cups water. Pour over chops. Spread rice evenly on top. Cover with apple, celery and onion. Bake, covered, at 350 degrees for 50 to 60 minutes or until chops are tender. Yield: 4 servings.

Mrs. Marsene Ham
Denver City, Texas

Sara Lu's Pork Chops and Wild Rice

3 to 4 pork chops
Salt and pepper to taste
1 10½-oz. can wild rice
1 can cream of mushroom soup
1 c. diced celery
Mushrooms (opt.)

Brown pork chops in skillet. Sprinkle with salt and pepper. Drain on paper towels. Mix remaining ingredients with 1 cup water in casserole. Place pork chops on top. Bake, covered, at 350 degrees for 30 minutes. Yield: 3-4 servings.

Sara Lu Greeley
Preston, Minnesota

Pork Chop-Wild Rice Casserole

1 c. herbed long grain and wild rice
6 pork chops
¼ c. almonds
½ c. mushrooms
½ c. chopped green pepper
¼ c. chopped onion
4 tbsp. butter
1 can cream of mushroom soup

Spread rice in greased 9 × 13-inch baking dish. Stir in 2½ cups boiling water. Bake at 350 degrees for 45 minutes. Brown pork chops in skillet. Cook over low heat until nearly tender. Saute next 4 ingredients in butter in small skillet until tender. Add vegetables and soup to rice; mix lightly. Arrange chops over rice. Bake for 30 minutes longer.

Carol Roberts
Oregon, Illinois

City Rice

1 c. rice
3 tbsp. olive oil
1 tsp. salt
3 cloves of garlic
3 tomatoes, chopped
1 c. chopped ripe and green olives
2 c. cooked diced pork

Brown rice in olive oil in skillet. Add salt, garlic, tomatoes and 2 cups boiling water. Simmer for 45 minutes or until done. Add olives and pork. Yield: 6-8 servings.

Augusta Jannett
Yoakum, Texas

Pork Hot Dish

1 lb. lean pork steak, cubed
1 can chicken soup
1 lb. noodles, cooked
1 1-lb. can whole kernel corn
½ lb. American cheese, diced
1 c. diced celery
¼ c. chopped pimento
Salt and pepper to taste
½ c. dry bread crumbs

Brown pork in skillet. Add soup and 1 soup can water. Simmer for 30 minutes. Add all ingredients except crumbs; mix well. Place in casserole. Sprinkle with crumbs. Bake at 350 degrees for 1 hour. Yield: 10 servings.

Mrs. Curtis Hardevidt
Jackson, Minnesota

Pork-Almond Scallop

1 lb. lean boneless pork, cubed
¾ lb. boneless veal, cubed
2 tbsp. butter
1 tsp. salt
1 can cream of mushroom soup
1 can cream of chicken soup
1 1-lb. package frozen French-fried
    potatoes
½ c. milk
½ c. sliced almonds
⅓ c. fine cereal crumbs

Brown pork and veal in butter in skillet over low heat. Add ¼ cup water and salt. Simmer, covered, for 1½ to 2 hours or until tender. Add soups, potatoes, milk and ¼ cup almonds; mix well. Spoon into shallow 2-quart casserole. Sprinkle with cereal crumbs and remaining almonds. Bake in 350-degree oven for 30 to 40 minutes or until heated through. Yield: 6 servings.

Helen Floyd
Lincoln, Nebraska

Pork-Noodle Treat

1½ lb. pork shoulder, cubed
1½ tsp. salt
Pepper to taste
Margarine
3 tbsp. flour
1 c. milk
3 oz. bleu cheese, crumbled
3 tbsp. each chopped green pepper,
    pimento
3 c. noodles, cooked

Brown pork in skillet. Season with ½ teaspoon salt and dash of pepper; remove. Add enough margarine to drippings to measure 3 tablespoons. Blend in flour and salt and pepper. Stir in milk. Cook until thick, stirring constantly. Add cheese, stirring to melt. Combine all ingredients; mix well. Pour into 6 × 10-inch baking dish. Bake at 350 degrees for 30 minutes. Yield: 6 servings.

Mary Jane Bertrand
Blackfoot, Idaho

Pork Savory

1 lb. lean pork
1½ tsp. salt
Dash of pepper
¾ c. sliced carrots
⅓ c. sifted flour
1 c. sour cream
1 c. diced potatoes
1 tsp. finely chopped onion
½ c. lima beans

Cut pork into 1-inch pieces; sprinkle with ½ teaspoon salt and pepper. Brown in skillet. Add 1 cup water. Simmer, covered, until pork is tender. Cook carrots in small amount of water until almost tender. Combine flour and sour cream in bowl; beat until smooth. Add to pork mixture. Add vegetables and remaining salt, blending well. Cover. Bake at 375 degrees for 1 hour. Remove cover. Bake for 30 minutes longer or until browned. Yield: 8 servings.

Grace Pylman
Clear Lake, South Dakota

Bacon-Macaroni Casserole

2 c. elbow macaroni
1 lb. bacon
½ c. chopped onion
¾ c. grated sharp cheese
1 can tomato soup
1 c. milk

Cook macaroni using package directions; drain. Reserve 4 slices bacon; cut remaining bacon into half-inch pieces. Brown cut bacon in skillet; drain. Cook onion in bacon drippings until soft; drain. Mix crisp bacon, macaroni, onion, cheese, soup and milk. Pour into greased casserole. Place reserved bacon slices on top. Bake at 375 degrees for 25 minutes or until bacon browns. Yield: 6 servings.

Lorene L. Arent
Wausa, Nebraska

Country Club Bacon and Eggs

12 slices bread, crusts removed
1 8-oz. package sharp Cheddar cheese, grated
1 8-oz. package Swiss cheese, grated
1 lb. Canadian bacon, thinly sliced
6 eggs, beaten
3 c. milk
½ tsp. salt

Alternate layers of bread slices, cheeses and bacon in 7 × 11-inch baking pan until all ingredients are used. Beat eggs with milk and salt in bowl. Pour over casserole. Cover. Refrigerate overnight. Bake at 325 degrees for 50 to 60 minutes.

Diane Webb
Ankeny, Iowa

Instant Bacon-Rice

10 slices bacon, cut up
1 med. onion, diced
2½ c. tomato juice
1 tsp. salt
½ tsp. pepper
2½ c. minute rice

Saute bacon and onion in skillet until bacon is crisp. Drain off half the drippings. Stir in next 3 ingredients. Bring to a boil. Add rice. Cover and remove from heat. Let stand for 5 minutes. Yield: 4-6 servings.

Donna E. Johnson
Saginaw, Michigan

Asparagus-Ham Casserole

1 lg. can asparagus
Milk
¼ c. minced onion
Butter
1 c. rice
2¼ c. broth
2 c. chopped ham
1 tbsp. flour
2 egg yolks, slightly beaten
Juice of 1 lemon

Drain asparagus, reserving liquid. Add enough milk to measure 1¼ cups liquid. Saute onion in ¾ stick butter in saucepan; add rice, stirring well. Add broth. Simmer, covered, until all liquid is absorbed, stirring occasionally. Place in 8 × 12-inch casserole. Layer with ham and asparagus. Melt 1 tablespoon butter in skillet; stir in flour until smooth. Add asparagus liquid; bring to a boil. Stir a small amount of hot mixture into egg yolks; stir egg yolks into hot mixture. Add lemon juice. Pour over casserole. Bake at 350 degrees for 20 minutes or until brown. Yield: 8 servings.

Leona Matson
Barstow, California

Baked Ham Salad

3 c. diced cooked ham
1 c. diced celery
½ c. chopped stuffed olives
2 hard-boiled eggs, chopped
2 tsp. minced onion
1 tbsp. lemon juice
2 tsp. mustard
Dash of pepper
¾ c. mayonnaise
1 c. crushed potato chips

Combine all ingredients except potato chips in large bowl; mix well. Place in 8-inch baking dish. Sprinkle with chips. Bake at 400 degrees for 20 to 25 minutes or until bubbly. Yield: 6 servings.

Sonja Crummy
Wyoming, Illinois

Golden Ham Pie

3 tbsp. chopped onion
¼ c. chopped green pepper
¼ c. butter
6 tbsp. flour
2 c. milk
2 c. diced cooked ham
1 can cream of chicken soup

Saute onions and green pepper in butter in skillet until tender. Blend in flour. Add milk, ham, and soup. Boil for 1 minute, stirring constantly. Pour into greased casserole. Bake at 450 degrees while preparing biscuits.

Cheese Biscuits

1 c. sifted flour
1½ tsp. baking powder
½ tsp. salt
2½ tsp. shortening
¾ c. grated cheese
1 pimento, chopped
⅓ c. milk

Sift first 3 ingredients into bowl. Cut in shortening until crumbly. Stir in remaining ingredients. Roll out on floured surface; cut with biscuit cutter. Place on casserole. Bake for 15 to 20 minutes longer or until brown. Yield: 4 servings.

Joyce Rapes
Sebewing, Michigan

Cheese Surprise

12 slices bread
¾ lb. sliced sharp process cheese
1 10-oz. package frozen chopped
     broccoli, cooked
2 c. diced ham
6 eggs, slightly beaten
3½ c. milk
¼ tsp. salt
1 tsp. dried onion flakes
½ tsp. dry mustard

Arrange half the bread in 9 × 13-inch baking dish. Layer cheese, broccoli and ham over bread. Top with remaining bread. Beat remaining ingredients together in bowl. Pour over layers. Refrigerate overnight. Bake at 325 degrees for 55 minutes or until brown.

Lois Brown
Blue River, Wisconsin

Gourmet Cheese and Ham Casserole

½ c. sliced celery
¼ c. chopped green pepper
1 c. milk
1 8-oz. package cream cheese, softened
½ tsp. salt
½ tsp. garlic salt
2 c. diced cooked ham
½ c. grated Parmesan cheese
½ lb. medium noodles, cooked, drained

Cook celery and green pepper in ½ cup boiling water in saucepan for 5 minutes; drain. Blend milk and cream cheese in saucepan until smooth. Warm over low heat, stirring constantly. Add seasonings, ham, cooked vegetables and half the cheese; mix well. Toss sauce lightly with noodles. Place in buttered 1½-quart casserole. Sprinkle with remaining cheese. Bake, covered, at 350 degrees for 30 to 35 minutes. Yield: 8 servings.

Sister M. Dorothy
Birmingham, Michigan

Ham Brunch Casserole

Butter
⅓ c. sifted flour
1 tsp. salt
2 c. milk
1 tbsp. instant onion
1 tsp. mustard

Dash of hot sauce
6 hard-boiled eggs, quartered
1 c. chopped ham
½ c. ripe olives
1 c. bread crumbs

Blend ¼ cup melted butter with next 3 ingredients in saucepan. Cook over low heat, stirring constantly, until thickened. Stir in next 3 ingredients. Layer next 3 ingredients in 1-quart casserole; add sauce. Melt 3 tablespoons butter in skillet; add bread crumbs. Toss to coat; arrange around edge of casserole. Garnish center with parsley. Bake at 375 degrees for ½ hour.

Ruth Natvig
Charles City, Iowa

Lynn's Ham and Cheese Casserole

1 c. diced cooked ham
1 c. cooked rice
1 c. grated Cheddar cheese
1 c. medium white sauce
Salt and pepper to taste

Combine ham, rice, ½ cup cheese, white sauce, salt and pepper in bowl; mix well. Place in greased casserole. Bake in 350-degree oven for 20 minutes. Top with remaining cheese.

Lynn Wagner
Newton, Mississippi

Hostess Special Casserole

1 c. slivered cooked ham
¼ c. chopped green pepper
¼ lb. mushrooms, quartered
Dash of thyme
2 tbsp. butter
1 can cream of chicken soup
2 c. cooked rice
1 9-oz. package frozen artichoke hearts,
     thawed
2 tbsp. Sherry
1 tbsp. chopped pimento
¼ c. shredded Cheddar cheese

Saute ham, green pepper and mushrooms with thyme in butter in skillet until green pepper is tender. Add remaining ingredients except cheese with ½ cup water; mix well. Spoon into 1½-quart casserole. Sprinkle cheese around edge. Bake at 350 degrees for 30 minutes.

Mrs. Emile E. Mugnani
Jamestown, Pennsylvania

Ham-Chicken Bake

½ c. chopped onion
½ c. chopped celery
¼ c. butter
¼ c. flour
1½ c. chicken broth
1½ c. light cream
2 c. diced cooked ham
2 c. diced cooked chicken
1 13-oz. can mushrooms, sliced
1 tsp. poultry seasoning
½ tsp. monosodium glutamate
¼ tsp. salt
Dash of pepper
Yam Biscuits

Saute onion and celery in butter in skillet until tender; blend in flour. Stir in broth and cream. Cook until mixture comes to a boil, stirring constantly. Add ham, chicken, mushrooms and seasonings; heat through. Pour into casserole. Drop Yam Biscuit dough around edge of casserole by tablespoonfuls. Bake at 350 degrees for 30 to 35 minutes.

Yam Biscuits

1 c. cooked mashed yams
⅓ c. melted butter
1 egg, beaten
1 c. sifted flour
2 tsp. baking powder
½ tsp. salt

Combine yams, butter and egg in bowl. Sift flour, baking powder and salt together; blend into yam mixture.

Mrs. Guy Mitchell
Chataignier, Louisiana

Ham and Eggs Au Gratin

2 tbsp. minced onion
6 tbsp. butter
6 tbsp. flour
½ tsp. salt
2½ c. milk
1½ c. shredded Cheddar cheese
6 hard-boiled eggs, sliced
2 c. cooked cubed potatoes
2 c. cooked cubed ham
2 tbsp. chopped parsley
Paprika

Cook onion in butter in skillet until tender. Blend in flour and salt. Cook until bubbly. Add milk. Cook, stirring constantly, until smooth and thickened. Add 1 cup cheese; stir until melted. Add eggs, potatoes, ham and parsley; mix well. Pour into 1½-quart baking dish; top with remaining cheese. Sprinkle with paprika. Bake at 350 degrees for 35 minutes or until top is lightly browned. Garnish with additional egg slices. Yield: 6 servings.

Jolene Douglas
Pocahontas, Iowa

Hunter's Dinner

1 4-oz. package spaghetti, cooked
2 c. whole kernel corn, drained
1 12-oz. package frozen lima beans, thawed
½ c. chili sauce
1 lb. bacon, diced
1 lb. cooked ham, diced

Combine first 4 ingredients in bowl; mix well. Brown bacon and ham in skillet over low heat; drain. Add to vegetable mixture; mix well. Pour into greased casserole. Bake at 350 degrees for 30 minutes.

Sister M. Tabitha Kaup
Omaha, Nebraska

Peachy Ham Pie

1 1-lb. can sliced peaches, drained
2 c. diced cooked ham
1 c. stuffing mix
1 c. finely chopped celery
2 eggs, slightly beaten
¼ c. French's Prepared Yellow Mustard
1 1¼-oz. envelope French's Cheese Sauce Mix

Set aside 8 to 10 peach slices; chop remaining slices. Combine chopped peaches with ham, stuffing mix, celery, eggs and mustard in large bowl. Prepare cheese sauce using package directions. Stir into ham mixture, mix well. Pour into greased 8-inch pie plate. Bake at 350 degrees for 25 minutes. Arrange sliced peaches on top of pie. Bake for 5 minutes longer. Yield: 4-6 servings.

Picture for this recipe on page 31.

Yam and Ham Casserole

1 tbsp. butter
1 med. orange, ground
½ c. whole cranberry sauce
½ c. maple syrup
2 16-oz. cans Louisiana yams, drained, sliced
1½ lb. cooked ham, cubed
½ c. chopped pecans
1 tbsp. brown sugar

Melt butter in saucepan. Stir in orange, cranberry sauce and syrup. Simmer over low heat for 5 minutes or until blended. Layer half the yams and half the ham in 2-quart casserole. Pour half the sauce over top. Add pecans to remaining sauce. Repeat yam and ham layers. Top with pecan sauce. Sprinkle with brown sugar. Bake at 350 degrees for 30 minutes.

Picture for this recipe on page 40.

Baked Eggs in Casserole

5 oz. boiled ham, thinly sliced
6 hard-boiled eggs, sliced
Salt to taste
1½ c. cream of chicken soup
2 tbsp. bread crumbs
½ c. grated Swiss cheese
Dash of paprika

Cut ham into thin strips. Alternate layers of ham and eggs in 1½-quart casserole. Add salt, and soup. Sprinkle with bread crumbs, cheese and paprika. Bake in 375-degree oven for 12 to 15 minutes or until bubbly and golden brown.

Anne Beatty Ransing
Miami, Florida

Vanessa's Ham Casserole

6 slices bread, trimmed, cubed
Baked ham slices
1 lb. cheese, sliced
3 eggs, beaten
½ tsp. salt
½ tsp. paprika
½ tsp. mustard
2½ c. milk

Alternate layers of bread cubes, ham and cheese in greased 1½-quart casserole, ending with cheese. Beat remaining ingredients together in bowl. Pour over casserole. Bake at 350 degrees for 1 hour or until set.

Vanessa Caulder
Germantown, Pennsylvania

Corene's Ham Casserole

4 med. potatoes, peeled, sliced
1 med. onion, chopped
Salt and pepper to taste
2 c. cooked green beans
1 slice cooked ham
⅓ c. bean liquid (opt.)

Place potatoes in buttered baking dish. Layer remaining ingredients in order given. Bake, covered, at 350 degrees for 1 hour or until potatoes are tender. Yield: 3-4 servings.

Corene Herbster
Lincoln, Nebraska

Ham-Turkey Supreme

1 2-lb canned ham, sliced
1 4 to 6-lb. cooked turkey breast, sliced
1 can golden mushroom soup
½ pt. sour cream
¼ c. Sherry
Salt and pepper to taste

Alternate layers of ham and turkey in casserole. Blend remaining ingredients together in bowl. Pour over ham and turkey. Bake at 250 degrees for 2 hours or until bubbly.

Mrs. B. Sachs
Thornwood, New York

Poultry

Broccoli-Chicken Divan

4 to 5 chicken breasts, boned, skinned
Salt
Pepper
1/8 tsp. sweet marjoram
1 tsp. instant bouillon
2 10-oz. packages broccoli spears frozen
    in butter sauce
2 12-oz. packages frozen rice pilaf
3 tbsp. butter
3 tbsp. flour
1½ c. milk
¾ c. shredded sharp American cheese

Place chicken in water to cover in large skillet. Add ½ teaspoon salt, ¼ teaspoon pepper and marjoram. Simmer, covered, for 40 to 45 minutes or until tender. Remove chicken. Add enough water to cooking liquid to measure 1 cup. Add bouillon. Bring to a boil; remove from heat. Cook broccoli and pilaf, using package directions. Turn rice into shallow 2-quart baking dish; fluff with fork. Add bouillon, stirring gently. Arrange broccoli on top. Place chicken over broccoli. Melt butter in medium saucepan. Blend in flour. Stir in milk gradually. Cook over medium heat until thickened, stirring constantly. Remove from heat. Add cheese and dash each of salt and pepper. Stir until cheese is melted. Pour ⅔ of the sauce over chicken. Bake, covered, at 350 degrees for 25 minutes. Serve with remaining sauce. Yield: 4-5 servings.

Picture for this recipe on page 41.

Chicken Breast Surprise

1 can cream of chicken soup
1 can cream of celery soup
¾ c. evaporated milk
¾ c. rice
6 chicken breasts
1 env. onion soup mix

Mix soups, milk and rice together in bowl. Place in shallow greased 2-quart baking dish. Arrange chicken breasts, skin side up, on rice mixture. Sprinkle with onion soup. Cover. Bake at 275 degrees for 2 hours. Yield: 6 servings.

Rita Bill
Johnson, Creek, Wisconsin

Chicken Divine

3 chicken breasts, cooked, boned
3 tbsp. flour
3 tbsp. butter, melted
1 can chicken broth
Salt and pepper to taste
½ c. grated Parmesan cheese
2 pkg. frozen broccoli spears, cooked

Cut chicken into large thin slices. Blend flour into butter in saucepan. Stir in broth. Cook over low heat until thick, stirring constantly. Blend in salt, pepper and ¼ cup cheese. Arrange broccoli in shallow casserole. Cover with chicken slices and sauce. Top with remaining cheese. Bake at 350 degrees for 20 minutes. Yield: 4 servings.

Susan Gonsoulin
Houma, Louisiana

Chicken and Dressing Bake

1 c. diced celery
⅔ c. minced onions
Butter
2 eggs, slightly beaten
3 c. milk
½ tsp. salt
¼ tsp. pepper
5 c. coarse bread crumbs
2-lb. chicken breasts
Seasoned flour

Saute celery and onions in 3 tablespoons butter in skillet for 5 minutes. Combine with next 5 ingredients in large bowl; mix well. Spoon lightly into 2-quart baking dish. Coat chicken with seasoned flour; brown in butter in skillet. Arrange chicken over dressing. Bake at 350 degrees for ½ hour. Cover with foil. Bake for 20 minutes. Remove foil. Bake for 10 minutes longer. Yield: 6 servings.

Catherine H. Maeder
Alva, Florida

Chicken Creole

1 fryer, cut up
2 tbsp. oil
1 onion, minced
1 green pepper, chopped
1 clove of garlic, minced
1 c. tomato paste
2 c. sliced okra

1 tbsp. vinegar
¾ tsp. salt
Pinch of allspice

Brown chicken in oil in skillet. Place in casserole. Mix onion, green pepper, garlic, tomato paste, okra, vinegar and seasonings in bowl. Pour over chicken. Cover. Bake in 350-degree oven for about 45 minutes.

Marjorie West
Lauderdale, Mississippi

Chicken and Artichoke Casserole

1 3-lb. fryer, cut up
1½ tsp. salt
¼ tsp. pepper
½ tsp. paprika
Butter
½ lb. mushrooms, sliced
2 tbsp. flour
⅔ c. chicken consomme
⅓ c. Sherry
1 12-oz. can artichoke hearts, drained
½ c. sliced pitted black olives
¼ c. chopped pimento

Sprinkle chicken with salt, pepper and paprika. Brown in butter in skillet. Place in large casserole. Saute mushrooms in 2 tablespoons butter in skillet. Sprinkle with flour. Stir in consomme and Sherry. Cook for 5 minutes, stirring frequently. Arrange artichoke hearts over chicken; cover with mushroom sauce. Garnish with olives and pimento. Bake, covered, at 375 degrees for 40 minutes. Yield: 6 servings.

Margaret Churchill
Manchester, Connecticut

Cripple Creek Chicken

½ c. minced onion
2 cloves of garlic, minced
½ c. margarine
2 tsp. paprika
1 fryer, cut up
Salt and pepper to taste
2 c. sour cream
¼ c. mayonnaise
½ c. Parmesan cheese
4 c. cooked buttered noodles

Saute onion and garlic in margarine in small skillet; add paprika. Season chicken with salt

and pepper. Roll in onion mixture. Arrange in 11 × 15-inch casserole. Spoon remaining onion mixture over chicken. Bake, covered, at 375 degrees for 40 minutes. Combine sour cream and mayonnaise with ¼ cup cheese; mix well. Combine ⅓ of sour cream mixture, chicken pan drippings and noodles in bowl; toss well. Layer noodles in casserole; add chicken. Top with remaining sour cream mixture and cheese. Bake at 325 degrees for ½ hour. Yield: 6-8 servings.

Holly Andrei
Cripple Creek, Colorado

Chicken-Mandarin Casserole

1 frying chicken, cut up
½ c. flour
1 tsp. salt
¼ tsp. pepper
⅓ c. oil
1 11-oz. can mandarin oranges
⅓ c. soy sauce
¼ c. packed brown sugar
½ tsp. nutmeg

Coat chicken with flour seasoned with salt and pepper. Brown in oil in large skillet. Place in shallow casserole. Drain oranges, reserving juice. Combine juice with remaining ingredients. Pour over chicken. Bake at 350 degrees for 40 minutes. Arrange orange pieces over chicken. Bake for 20 minutes longer. Yield: 6-8 servings.

Joalene Sepke
Mt. Clemens, Michigan

Chicken-Chili Casserole

1 med. onion, chopped
1 clove of garlic, minced
3 c. white sauce
1 or 2 cans green chili
1 doz. corn tortillas, torn into strips
1 chicken, cooked, boned, chopped
¾ lb. Cheddar cheese, grated

Saute onion and garlic in skillet until golden. Add white sauce and green chili, mixing well. Alternate layers of tortillas, chicken, sauce and cheese in buttered casserole until all ingredients are used. Bake at 350 degrees for 35 minutes or until bubbly. Yield: 10 servings.

Linda Carol Gillum
Mineral Wells, Texas

Chicken-Asparagus Casserole

6 tbsp. butter
½ c. flour
2 c. chicken broth
1 c. mayonnaise
½ tsp. curry powder
1 tbsp. lemon juice
1 can asparagus
1 chicken, cooked, boned, diced

Blend butter and flour in saucepan over low heat; stir in broth gradually. Add next 3 ingredients. Cook over medium heat until thickened, stirring frequently. Line casserole with asparagus, reserving some for garnish. Add chicken; cover with sauce. Top with reserved asparagus. Bake at 350 degrees for 30 minutes.

Patricia Morgan
Laurel, Montana

Chicken-Cashew Casserole

2 c. cubed cooked chicken
2 c. thinly sliced celery
½ c. cashews (opt.)
½ tsp. salt
2 tsp. grated onion
2 tsp. lemon juice
1 c. mayonnaise
1 sm. can mushrooms, drained (opt.)
½ c. grated American cheese
1 c. crushed potato chips

Toss chicken with all ingredients except cheese and potato chips. Place in casserole. Sprinkle cheese and potato chips on top. Bake at 450 degrees for 10 to 20 minutes. Yield: 6 servings.

M. Judelle Jones
Turlock, California

Chicken Crunch

½ c. milk
2 c. chicken broth
Butter, softened
6 tbsp. flour
Dash of nutmeg
Dash of celery salt
2½ c. chopped cooked chicken
1 c. zwieback crumbs
Slivered almonds

Heat first two ingredients together in saucepan. Combine ¼ cup butter, flour, nutmeg and celery salt together in bowl; blend well. Stir butter mixture into hot mixture. Cook over low heat until smooth and creamy, stirring constantly. Alternate layers of chicken, sauce and crumbs in 8-inch square baking dish until all ingredients are used. Dot with butter. Sprinkle almonds over top. Bake at 350 degrees for 20 to 30 minutes or until bubbly.

Alice Applegate
Knoxville, Iowa

Chicken-Crab Rosemary

2 tbsp. chopped onion
½ c. butter
7 tbsp. flour
¾ tsp. salt
¾ tsp. paprika
1 tsp. crushed rosemary
2 c. chicken broth
2 c. sour cream
3 c. chopped cooked chicken
2 6½-oz. cans flaked crab meat
1½ c. avocado chunks
Lemon juice
1 c. coarse buttered toast crumbs

Saute onion in butter in saucepan until golden. Blend in flour, salt, paprika and rosemary. Heat until bubbly. Remove from heat. Add chicken broth gradually. Bring to a boil. Cook for 2 minutes, stirring constantly. Remove from heat. Blend in sour cream gradually. Add chicken and crab meat. Sprinkle avocado with lemon juice. Add to crab meat; mix well. Place in buttered casserole. Cover with crumbs. Bake at 350 degrees for 30 minutes.

Laura Lynn Porter
Boron, California

Chicken Diablo

2½ lb. chicken breasts and thighs, cooked
1 lg. bell pepper, diced
1 c. chopped celery
¼ lb. butter
3 tbsp. flour
3 tbsp. cooking Sherry
1 tsp. hot sauce
1 can cream of mushroom soup
½ c. milk
2 hard-boiled eggs, chopped
Salt and pepper to taste
½ tsp. minced garlic
Grated cheese

Bone and chop chicken; set aside. Saute bell pepper and celery in butter in skillet until tender. Add flour, chicken and remaining ingredients except cheese; mix well. Place in casserole. Top with cheese. Bake at 350 degrees for 1 hour. Yield: 6 servings.

Flossie G. Richards
Lafayette, Alabama

Chicken and Dressing Casserole

2 tsp. minced onion
6 tsp. butter
½ tsp. celery salt
1 tsp. salt
1 tsp. sage
Pepper to taste
3 to 4 c. soft bread crumbs
1 4 to 5-lb. chicken, cooked, boned
⅓ c. shortening
⅓ c. flour
6 c. chicken broth
6 eggs, well beaten
Dried bread crumbs

Saute onion in butter in large skillet. Add next 5 ingredients; toss lightly to mix. Spread in greased baking dish. Arrange chicken over dressing. Melt shortening in saucepan; blend in flour. Stir in broth. Cook for 5 minutes, stirring constantly. Cool slightly; blend in eggs. Cook for 3 minutes, stirring constantly. Pour over chicken. Top with dried bread crumbs. Bake at 350 degrees for 1 hour or until brown. Yield: 12 servings.

Eleanor Howard
Kent, Washington

Chicken and Stuffing Scallop

1¾ c. herb-seasoned stuffing mix
1½ c. cubed cooked chicken
¼ c. butter
¼ c. flour
Salt and pepper to taste
2 c. chicken broth
3 eggs, slightly beaten

Prepare stuffing using package directions. Spread in 6 × 10-inch baking dish. Arrange chicken over stuffing. Melt butter in saucepan. Blend in flour, salt and pepper. Add broth. Cook, stirring constantly, until thick. Stir a small amount of hot mixture into eggs; stir eggs into hot mixture. Blend well. Pour over

chicken. Bake at 325 degrees for 35 to 40 minutes or until knife inserted in center comes out clean. Let stand for 5 minutes. Yield: 6 servings.

Mary S. Sodergren
Annandale, Virginia

Company Chicken Casserole

2 c. cubed chicken
2 c. chopped celery
½ c. blanched slivered almonds
1 c. water chestnuts, quartered
½ c. grated Cheddar cheese
2 tbsp. minced green onion
½ tsp. seasoned salt
⅛ tsp. white pepper
2 tbsp. lemon juice
Mayonnaise
½ tsp. Worcestershire sauce
1 jar small button mushrooms
2 hard-boiled eggs, quartered
½ c. fine dry bread crumbs
2 tbsp. melted butter
¼ c. grated Parmesan cheese

Combine first 8 ingredients in large bowl; toss lightly. Add lemon juice, Worcestershire sauce and enough mayonnaise to moisten. Spoon into buttered 8 × 13-inch baking dish. Arrange mushrooms and eggs over top. Combine bread crumbs, butter and cheese in small bowl. Sprinkle over chicken mixture. Bake at 350 degrees for 15 to 20 minutes or until bubbly. Yield: 6-8 servings.

Ruth Cooper
Culver City, California

King Ranch Casserole Delight

1 can tortillas, cut in pieces
1 c. cooked diced chicken
1 can tomatoes with green chilies
1 med. onion, chopped
1 c. chicken broth
1 can cream of mushroom soup
1 can cream of chicken soup
1 c. shredded Cheddar cheese

Combine all ingredients except cheese in casserole, mixing well. Top with cheese. Refrigerate for 8 hours. Bake at 350 degrees for ¾ hour. Yield: 6-8 servings.

Jane Wheeler
Waco, Texas

¼ c. chopped pimento
3½ c. French-fried onions
Paprika

Combine first 9 ingredients and 3 cups French-fried onions in large bowl; mix well. Place in greased 1½-quart casserole. Cover. Bake at 350 degrees for 30 minutes. Top with remaining ½ cup onions. Sprinkle with paprika. Bake, uncovered, for 5 minutes longer.

Evangeline Maxwell
Spencer, Iowa

Maine Chicken Curry

1 4 to 5-lb. chicken
Garlic salt to taste
Celery salt to taste
Bay leaves to taste
Salt and pepper to taste
3 or 4 med. onions, peeled
2 pkg. frozen broccoli spears
2 cans cream of celery soup
1 c. mayonnaise
¼ c. lemon juice
5 tsp. curry powder

Place first 6 ingredients in large saucepan with enough water to cover. Simmer until chicken is tender. Remove meat from bones; chop coarsely. Cook broccoli according to package directions for ½ required time. Place in buttered 9 × 13-inch baking dish. Place chicken over broccoli. Combine remaining ingredients in small bowl; mix well. Pour over chicken. Bake at 350 degrees for 30 minutes. Garnish with pimento strips.

Pauline Webster
Lincoln, Maine

Lemon-Chicken Casserole

1 8-oz. package frozen green peas and
    potatoes with cream sauce
2 tsp. lemon juice
1½ c. diced cooked chicken
1 c. herb-seasoned stuffing mix
¼ tsp. thyme opt.
1 tsp. lemon rind

Prepare peas and potatoes according to package directions, using 1 cup water. Add lemon juice and chicken; mix well. Pour into 1-quart casserole. Prepare stuffing using package directions. Add thyme and lemon rind. Spoon over casserole. Bake at 350 degrees for 10 minutes or until bubbly. Garnish with lemon slices and parsley. Yield: 3-4 servings.

Picture for this recipe above.

Gourmet Chicken Casserole

2 c. diced chicken
1 c. diced celery
½ c. salted cashews
3 tbsp. lemon juice
½ c. chopped green pepper
¼ tsp. salt
1 c. mayonnaise
½ c. milk

Sherry's Baked Chicken Casserole

¼ c. flour
2 c. skim milk
2 chicken bouillon cubes
1 c. elbow macaroni, cooked
2 c. diced cooked chicken
½ tsp. marjoram
Dash of pepper
¼ c. chopped parsley
¼ c. chopped onion
1 c. diced celery
1 3-oz. can mushrooms (opt.)
2 tbsp. chopped green pepper
2 tsp. salt

Blend flour and milk in saucepan. Add boullion cubes. Cook until thick, stirring constantly. Stir in remaining ingredients. Pour into casserole. Bake at 350 degrees for 30 minutes or until bubbly. Yield: 5 servings.

Sherry Zeigler
Chillicothe, Ohio

Caribbean Chicken

1 pkg. macaroni and cheese dinner
1 c. cubed cooked chicken
½ c. chopped ripe olives
⅓ c. sour cream
2 tbsp. chopped parsley

Prepare dinner using package directions. Add remaining ingredients; mix well. Place in casserole. Bake in 350-degree oven for 30 minutes. Yield: 6 servings.

Echo P. Schepman
North Bend, Oregon

Chicken Delicious

3 tbsp. butter
3 tbsp. flour
1 tsp. salt
3 c. chicken broth
4 c. chopped cooked chicken
8 hard-boiled eggs, chopped
1 pkg. frozen peas, cooked
1 4-oz. can mushroom pieces
3 c. macaroni, cooked
½ c. buttered bread crumbs

Melt butter in medium saucepan. Add flour and salt. Add chicken broth slowly, stirring constantly. Cook over low heat until thickened, stirring constantly. Remove from heat. Stir in chicken, eggs, peas, mushrooms and macaroni. Pour into shallow greased 2-quart casserole. Top with bread crumbs. Bake at 350 degrees for 30 minutes. Yield: 10 servings.

Ghlee Kershner
Montpelier, Indiana

Chicken Finale

¼ c. chopped green pepper
¼ c. minced onion
2 tbsp. butter
1 can cream of chicken soup

1 c. sour cream
¼ c. milk
¼ c. sliced ripe olives
½ tsp. salt
¼ tsp. pepper
1½ c. diced cooked chicken
2 c. medium noodles, cooked
¼ c. quartered blanched almonds
1 tbsp. minced parsley

Saute green pepper and onion in butter in large skillet until tender. Stir in next 8 ingredients. Pour into greased 1½-quart casserole. Sprinkle with almonds and parsley. Bake at 350 degrees for 35 minutes or until bubbly. Yield: 6 servings.

Gail Kelly
Clearfield, Pennsylvania

Chicken-Noodle Casserole

2 c. chopped cooked chicken
½ c. chopped celery
½ c. mayonnaise
¼ c. slivered almonds
3 hard-boiled eggs, chopped
1 tbsp. lemon juice
2 c. chicken gravy
1 sm. can Chinese noodles

Mix all ingredients except noodles in casserole. Top with noodles. Bake at 375 degrees until bubbly. Yield: 4-6 servings.

Mary Smithwich
Coltrane, North Dakota

Chicken-Pecan Casserole

1 lg. package egg noodles
1 stewing chicken, cooked, boned, diced
2 cans cream of mushroom soup
2 tbsp. pimento
½ c. pecans
2 c. chicken broth
Buttered bread crumbs

Cook noodles using package directions until nearly tender. Combine with remaining ingredients except crumbs; mix well. Place in casserole. Top with crumbs. Bake at 350 degrees for ½ hour. Yield: 8 servings.

Billye D. Freeland
El Paso, Texas

Chicken-Almond Casserole

2 c. chopped cooked chicken
1 can chicken soup
½ c. mayonnaise
1 c. chopped celery
½ c. chopped onion
1 tbsp. lemon juice
1 c. cooked rice
½ c. slivered almonds
Salt and pepper to taste
Rice Krispies

Combine all ingredients except Rise Krispies in large bowl; mix well. Pour into greased baking dish. Top with Rice Krispies. Bake at 350 degrees for 30 minutes. Yield: 6 servings.

Wilma Tucker
Marion, Louisiana

Chicken and Rice Au Gratin

¾ c. margarine
¾ c. flour
1½ qt. chicken stock
1 qt. cubed cooked chicken
1 c. light cream
1 tsp. Worcestershire sauce
1 tbsp. salt
¼ tsp. pepper
2½ lb. rice, cooked
2 c. grated cheese
3 c. buttered bread crumbs

Melt margarine in large saucepan. Blend in flour to make smooth paste. Add chicken stock gradually. Cook until thickened, stirring constantly. Add chicken, cream, Worcestershire sauce, salt and pepper; mix well. Alternate layers of rice and chicken mixture in large baking dish. Sprinkle with cheese and crumbs. Bake at 450 degrees for 20 minutes. Yield: 50 servings.

Zelota Yates
Raleigh, North Carolina

Club Chicken Casserole

¼ c. flour
¼ c. butter, melted
1 c. chicken broth
1 14½-oz. can evaporated milk
1½ tsp. salt
3 c. cooked rice
2½ c. diced cooked chicken

1 3-oz. can broiled sliced mushrooms, drained
¼ c. chopped pimento
⅓ c. chopped green pepper
½ c. blanched toasted almonds, slivered

Combine flour and butter in large saucepan; stir until smooth. Add broth, milk and ½ cup water. Cook over low heat until thick and smooth, stirring constantly. Add remaining ingredients except almonds; mix well. Pour into greased 12 × 8-inch baking dish. Bake at 350 degrees for 30 minutes. Top with almonds. Yield: 8 servings.

Patricia Edwards
Wilson, North Carolina

Chicken-Rice Casserole

4 c. diced cooked chicken
2 c. (scant) soft bread crumbs
1 c. rice, cooked
½ c. diced pimento
4 eggs, beaten
1 tbsp. salt
¼ c. melted butter
3 c. chicken broth

Combine all ingredients in large bowl; mix well. Place in casserole. Bake at 325 degrees for 2 hours. Yield: 8 servings.

Mrs. Lewis Vance
Jefferson, Pennsylvania

Dilled Chicken Casserole

2 10-oz. packages frozen broccoli spears, thawed, drained
½ lb. fresh mushrooms, sliced
¾ c. chopped onions
1 med. clove of garlic, crushed
⅓ c. butter
2 cans chicken gravy
3 c. cooked rice
2 c. cubed cooked chicken
2 c. sliced celery
2 tbsp. dry Sherry
¾ tsp. dillweed, crushed
¼ tsp. salt
¼ tsp. white pepper

Trim broccoli flowerets; reserve for garnish. Chop stalks coarsely; set aside. Saute mushrooms, onions and garlic in butter in large skillet until onions are tender. Stir in remaining ingredients. Cook over low heat for 5 minutes, stirring constantly. Pour into 3-quart casserole. Bake, covered, at 400 degrees for 30 minutes. Uncover; garnish with reserved broccoli. Bake for 10 minutes longer. Yield: 6 servings.

Bobbie Jo Smith
Brunton, Georgia

Mushroom-Chicken Casserole

2 c. cooked rice
½ c. milk
2 c. chopped cooked chicken
1 c. mushrooms, drained
1 pimento, sliced
½ c. grated cheese

Combine all ingredients except cheese in bowl; mix well. Spoon into buttered baking dish. Bake at 350 degrees for 27 minutes. Sprinkle with grated cheese. Bake for 3 minutes longer. Yield: 6 servings.

Mary Pinkston Whaley
Northport, Alabama

Oriental Chicken Casserole

1 c. minute rice
1 can water chestnuts, drained, sliced
½ c. salad dressing
1 can cream of chicken soup
1 onion, grated
1 pkg. frozen green beans, thawed
2 c. cooked diced chicken
Buttered crumbs
Parmesan cheese (opt.)

Prepare rice using package directions. Add remaining ingredients except crumbs and cheese; mix well. Pour into casserole. Top with crumbs and cheese. Bake at 350 degrees for 30 minutes. Yield: 4 to 6 servings.

Sue Stephens
Wheatland, Wyoming

Sherried Mushroom Chicken

2 3-lb. broiler-fryers
1 c. dry Sherry
1½ tsp. salt
½ tsp. curry powder
1 med. onion, sliced

½ c. sliced celery
1 lb. fresh mushrooms
¼ c. butter
2 6-oz. packages long grain and wild rice
  with seasonings
1 c. sour cream
1 can cream of mushroom soup

Place first 6 ingredients and 1 cup water in deep kettle. Bring to a boil; cover. Simmer over low heat for 1 hour. Bone and chop chicken. Strain broth; set aside. Saute mushrooms until golden brown. Cook rice according to package directions, using strained broth as part of liquid. Combine chicken, rice and half the mushrooms in large bowl. Blend sour cream and soup in small bowl. Add to chicken mixture; toss lightly. Pour into baking dish. Garnish with remaining mushrooms. Bake at 350 degrees for 1 hour. Yield: 8 to 10 servings.

Violet Mosely
Avon Park, Florida

Spicy Hot Chicken Salad

⅛ tsp. ginger
¼ tsp. garlic powder
Pepper to taste
⅓ c. white wine
3 tbsp. lemon juice
½ tsp. nutmeg
4 whole chicken breasts
9 hard-boiled eggs, chopped
½ c. chopped onion
¼ tsp. basil
¼ tsp. rosemary
¾ c. slivered almonds
2 cans cream of celery soup
1 can cream of chicken soup
1½ c. mayonnaise
1⅓ c. finely crushed potato chips

Combine first 5 ingredients with ¼ teaspoon nutmeg in bowl; mix well. Place chicken in baking pan; pour wine mixture over top. Bake, covered, at 325 degrees until tender. Cool in pan juices. Debone chicken; chop coarsely. Combine with remaining ingredients, reserving ⅔ cup potato chips; mix well. Place in casserole. Top with reserved potato chips. Bake at 350 degrees for 30 to 35 minutes.

Linda Bailey
Powhatan, Virginia

Chicken-Spaghetti Casserole

1¼ c. broken spaghetti
1 tsp. salt
1½ c. chopped boiled chicken
¼ c. pimento, finely chopped
1 lg. green pepper, finely chopped
1 onion, finely chopped
1 sm. can mushrooms
1 c. chicken broth
1¾ c. shredded cheese

Cook spaghetti using package directions. Combine with remaining ingredients; mix well. Pour into greased casserole. Bake at 350 degrees for 1 hour. Yield: 8-10 servings.

Inez P. Curvin
Alexander City, Alabama

Chicken Tetrazzini

1 7-oz. package spaghetti
Chicken broth
1 stalk celery, chopped, cooked, drained
1 med. green pepper, minced
2 med. onions, minced
1 5 to 6-lb. chicken, cooked, boned, chopped
¾ lb. margarine
1 c. flour
4 c. milk
1 lb. American cheese, grated
1 can cream of mushroom soup
Salt and pepper to taste
Garlic salt (opt.)
Paprika
1 box Ritz cracker crumbs

Cook spaghetti in chicken broth using package directions. Combine with next 4 ingredients. Melt ½ pound margarine in large saucepan. Blend in flour until smooth. Stir in milk; blend well. Cook until thick, stirring constantly. Add cheese and soup; blend until smooth. Season. Combine with spaghetti, mixing well. Pour into baking dish. Melt remaining margarine; toss with crumbs. Sprinkle over casserole. Bake at 350 degrees for ½ hour. Yield: 15-20 servings.

Susie Tucker
Savoy, Texas

Scalloped Chicken Casserole

1 egg, lightly beaten
½ tsp. salt
¼ tsp. pepper
1 8-oz. can cream-style corn
1 10-oz. package frozen chopped broccoli, partially thawed
3½ c. diced cooked chicken
¼ c. melted butter
2 c. herb-seasoned stuffing mix
2 c. chicken broth
¼ c. flour
¼ tsp. sage

Combine first 5 ingredients in bowl; mix well. Spread in greased 9 × 14-inch baking dish. Add chicken to vegetables. Toss butter and stuffing mix together; spread over chicken. Blend remaining ingredients together in saucepan. Cook until thick, stirring constantly. Pour over casserole. Bake at 325 degrees for 25 minutes or until bubbly. Yield: 6-8 servings.

Alma Lee Hicks
Murphysboro, Illinois

Cornish Hen Casserole

6 Cornish hens, split
Flour
Salt
Paprika
½ c. Wesson oil
3 c. instant rice
1 c. wild rice
1 can celery soup
1 can chicken soup
Parsley flakes
1 pkg. frozen English peas, thawed

Coat Cornish hens with flour seasoned with salt and paprika. Brown Cornish hens in oil in skillet. Combine instant rice and wild rice. Spread in buttered shallow casserole. Combine soups with 2 soup cans water in saucepan. Bring to a boil. Pour over rice; mix well. Place Cornish hens, cut side down, on rice. Top with parsley flakes. Bake at 350 degrees for 1½ hours. Arrange peas around edge of casserole. Bake for 30 minutes longer.

LaVerne Stokes
Lakewood, Colorado

Flowering Plum Cornish Hens

4 Cornish hens, split
1 tsp. seasoned salt
2 lg. oranges, sliced
¼ c. margarine, melted
¼ c. diced onion
1 tsp. ginger
1 tsp. Worcestershire sauce
1½ tsp. mustard
⅓ c. chili sauce
¼ c. soy sauce
1 6-oz. can frozen lemonade, thawed
1 1-lb. can purple plums, pureed
¼ c. shredded coconut

Sprinkle Cornish hens with seasoned salt. Arrange orange slices in shallow roasting pan. Place Cornish hens, skin side up, over oranges. Bake at 350 degrees for 45 minutes. Combine next 9 ingredients in saucepan; blend well. Simmer for 15 minutes, stirring frequently. Pour plum sauce over Cornish hens. Bake for 20 minutes longer, basting frequently. Arrange on heated platter. Spoon pan drippings over top. Sprinkle with coconut. Yield: 4-6 servings.

Frances Baratz
Waterford, Connecticut

Italian Cornish Hens and Rice

1 c. long grain rice
1 env. Italian salad dressing mix
1 can cream of chicken soup
2 Cornish hens, halved
Salt and pepper to taste (opt.)

Spread rice in shallow 3-quart casserole. Bake at 350 degrees for 15 minutes or until golden, stirring occasionally. Combine dressing mix, 2½ cups boiling water and soup in bowl; stir into rice. Season Cornish hens with salt and pepper. Place cut side down on rice. Cover tightly with foil. Bake for 1 hour. Remove cover. Bake for 30 minutes longer or until rice and Cornish hens are tender.

Beverly Cederstrom
Lindstrom, Minnesota

Cheddary Turkey Casserole

4 oz. broad noodles, cooked
2½ c. diced cooked turkey
1 4½-oz. jar whole mushrooms, drained
1 tbsp. instant minced onion

1 c. milk
1 11-oz. can Cheddar cheese soup
1 c. finely crushed cheese crackers
3 tbsp. butter, melted

Place noodles in greased 2-quart casserole. Cover with turkey and mushrooms. Combine onion, milk and soup in bowl; mix well. Pour over mushrooms. Mix cracker crumbs and butter; sprinkle over casserole. Bake at 350 degrees for 35 minutes.

Delores Vondrak
Elk Point, South Dakota

Crunchy Turkey Strata

1½ cans chow mein noodles
1 can water chestnuts, sliced
3 or 4 stalks celery, sliced thin
2 c. diced cooked turkey
2 cans cream of mushroom soup
1 med. onion, minced
½ c. broken cashews

Spread half the noodles in buttered 2-quart casserole. Combine next 5 ingredients in bowl with ½ soup can water; mix well. Spread over noodles. Sprinkle remaining noodles over top. Bake at 350 degrees for 40 minutes. Top with cashews. Bake for 20 minutes longer. Yield: 6 servings.

Karin Bargar
Lansing, Michigan

Tater Turkey

1 c. mayonnaise
2 tbsp. minced green pepper
2 tbsp. chopped celery
2 tbsp. chopped pimento
3 hard-boiled eggs, chopped
4 c. seasoned mashed potatoes
2 c. chopped cooked turkey
½ c. grated cheese

Combine first 5 ingredients in bowl. Layer half the potatoes in greased 9 × 3-inch casserole. Add turkey. Cover with sauce. Top with remaining potatoes. Sprinkle with cheese. Bake at 350 degrees for ½ hour or until light brown. Yield: 6-8 servings.

Mrs. R. H. Russell
McCormick, S. C.

Deep-Dish Turkey Pie

6 med. potatoes, peeled, quartered
6 med. carrots, peeled, quartered
1 sm. onion, chopped
¼ c. chopped green pepper
6 tbsp. butter
1 can cream of chicken soup
3 c. diced cooked turkey
1½ c. sifted flour
2 tsp. baking powder
½ tsp. salt
Milk

Cook potatoes and carrots in large saucepan until tender. Drain, reserving 1 cup liquid. Saute onion and green pepper in 2 tablespoons butter in medium saucepan until soft. Stir in soup and reserved liquid. Spoon potatoes and carrots into 8-cup casserole. Pour onion sauce over top. Bake at 425 degrees for 15 minutes. Sift dry ingredients together in bowl. Cut in remaining butter. Add ½ cup milk. Stir until blended. Knead lightly on floured surface. Roll out to ½-inch thickness. Cut with 2-inch biscuit cutter. Brush tops of biscuits with milk. Arrange biscuits on top of turkey mixture. Bake for 15 minutes longer or until biscuits are golden brown.

Ruth Riale
Bloomsburg, Pennsylvania

Delicious Turkey Casserole

1 can cream of chicken soup
½ c. mayonnaise
¾ c. chicken bouillon
2 tbsp. lemon juice
2 tbsp. finely chopped onion
1 c. chopped blanched almonds
1 tbsp. chopped parsley
½ tsp. salt
½ tsp. white pepper
1 c. finely chopped celery
3 hard-boiled eggs, chopped fine
2 c. chopped cooked turkey
1 c. cracker crumbs

Combine first 9 ingredients in bowl; mix well. Stir in celery, eggs and turkey. Place in greased 2-quart casserole. Top with cracker crumbs. Bake at 325 degrees for 30 minutes or until bubbly. Yield: 6 servings.

Sarah P. Bowles
Holladay, Tennessee

Turkey and Brown Rice Casserole

3 c. cooked turkey
3½ c. cooked brown rice
1 c. chopped onion
1 c. sliced celery
1 c. chopped green pepper
3 tbsp. butter
1 can cream of mushroom soup
½ c. dry white wine
1 6-oz. can sliced mushrooms
1 tsp. sage
¼ tsp. thyme
½ tsp. salt
Dash of pepper
1 4-oz. can pimento, drained, chopped
1 c. herb-seasoned croutons

Combine turkey and rice in greased 2½-quart casserole. Saute onion, celery and green pepper in 2 tablespoons butter in large skillet until tender-crisp, stirring frequently. Stir in next 8 ingredients. Pour over turkey, stirring to mix well. Melt remaining butter in skillet. Add croutons; toss until coated. Spoon around casserole. Bake at 350 degrees for 40 minutes or until bubbly.

Virginia Lund
Cedar Falls, Iowa

Turkey-Cranberry Squares

2 tbsp. butter
½ c. sugar
1 tsp. grated orange peel
2 c. fresh cranberries
5 c. ground cooked turkey
1 c. turkey stock
1 c. milk
1 tsp. salt
¼ tsp. pepper
2 tbsp. finely chopped onion
2 c. soft bread crumbs
2 eggs, slightly beaten

Melt butter in 8-inch baking dish. Blend in sugar and orange peel. Cover with cranberries. Combine remaining ingredients in bowl; mix well. Press firmly over cranberries. Bake at 400 degrees for 45 minutes. Turn out upside down onto serving platter. Cut into squares. Yield: 8 servings.

M. Christiana Gates
Middleboro, Massachusetts

Seafood

Haddock-Shrimp Bake

1 can shrimp, drained
2 lb. frozen haddock, thawed
1 can shrimp soup
¼ c. melted margarine
1 tsp. grated onion
½ tsp. Worcestershire sauce
¼ tsp. garlic salt
1¼ c. crushed Ritz crackers

Place shrimp and haddock in greased 13 × 9 × 2-inch baking dish. Spread with soup. Bake in 375-degree oven for 20 minutes. Combine remaining ingredients; sprinkle over fish mixture. Bake for 10 minutes longer. Yield: 6 servings.

Connie Phillips
Fenton, Michigan

Baked Fish with Tomato Sauce

2 pkg. frozen fish fillets, partially thawed
2 tbsp. minced onion
1 clove of garlic, minced
1 tbsp. butter
2 8-oz. cans tomato sauce
1 tsp. sugar
½ tsp. Worcestershire sauce
2 tbsp. lemon juice
Chopped Parsley (opt.)

Cut fish into 6 portions. Arrange in greased shallow baking dish. Saute onion and garlic in butter in skillet until tender. Add remaining ingredients except parsley. Simmer for 5 minutes. Pour over fish. Bake at 400 degrees for 20 to 25 minutes. Sprinkle with chopped parsley. Yield: 6 servings.

Eva Jane Schwartz
Gettysburg, Pennsylvania

Baked Fish with Vegetables

1 lb. fish
1 tbsp. salt
1 tbsp. pepper
1 12-oz. can mixed vegetables, drained
2 sm. onions, thinly sliced
2 sm. tomatoes, thinly sliced
4 slices bacon

Place fish in greased baking dish; sprinkle with salt and pepper. Spread mixed vegetables over fish. Place onion and tomato slices over vegetables; sprinkle lightly with salt and pepper. Top with bacon. Bake at 400 degrees for 30 to 45 minutes or until fish flakes easily. Yield: 4 servings.

Gladys S. Hendren
Holly Hill, Florida

Cheese-Fish Bake

1 lb. fish fillets
1 can cream of mushroom soup
Dash of pepper
¼ c. shredded Cheddar cheese
Dash of paprika

Arrange fish in greased 10 × 6 × 2-inch baking dish. Pour soup over fish. Sprinkle with pepper, cheese and paprika. Bake at 375 degrees for 45 minutes or until lightly browned. Yield: 4-6 servings.

Katherine Reddeman
Chelsea, Michigan

Codfish Souffle

1 c. codfish, rinsed, drained
2 c. mashed potatoes
2 c. milk
2 eggs, well beaten
½ c. butter, melted
Salt and pepper to taste

Combine all ingredients in bowl; mix thoroughly. Place in baking dish. Bake at 300 degrees for about 30 minutes. Yield: 4 servings.

Mary Jane Bertrand
Blackfoot, Idaho

Creole Haddock

2 lb. haddock fillets
1½ c. chopped fresh tomatoes
½ c. chopped green pepper
⅓ c. lemon juice
1 tbsp. safflower oil
2 tsp. salt
2 tsp. instant minced onion
1 tsp. crushed basil leaves
¼ tsp. coarse black pepper
4 drops of hot sauce

Place fillets in 13½ × 9 × 2-inch baking dish. Combine remaining ingredients; spoon over fillets. Bake at 500 degrees for 5 to 8 minutes.

Avis Henning
Miltonvale, Kansas

Fish Baked in Onion Sauce

3 c. sliced onions
1/3 c. butter
4 tbsp. flour
1 tsp. salt
2 c. milk
1 lb. fish fillets
1/2 c. dry buttered bread crumbs

Saute onions in butter in skillet until golden. Blend in flour and salt. Stir in milk. Cook until thick, stirring constantly. Place fish in greased 6 × 10-inch baking dish. Cover with sauce. Top with crumbs. Bake at 375 degrees for 30 minutes. Yield: 5 servings.

Donna Bingaman
Mifflinburg, Pennsylvania

Halibut Au Gratin

2 tbsp. butter
2 tbsp. flour
1 1/2 tsp. salt
1/2 tsp. pepper
1 c. hot milk
1/2 c. celery, minced
2 lb. halibut steaks
2 c. cheese, grated
1/2 c. buttered crumbs

Melt butter in saucepan. Blend in flour, salt and pepper. Stir in milk. Cook until thick, stirring constantly. Add celery. Alternate layers of halibut, sauce and cheese in buttered baking dish until all ingredients are used. Top with crumbs. Bake at 350 degrees for 1 hour. Yield: 8 servings.

Margaret Schlotz
Waldport, Oregon

Curried Salmon with Cheese Pinwheels

1 10-oz. package frozen mixed
    vegetables, cooked
1 1-lb. can salmon, drained
1 can cream of mushroom soup
1/4 tsp. salt
1/4 tsp. curry powder
1/4 tsp. pepper
Milk
2 c. prepared biscuit mix
1/2 c. shredded sharp cheese

Mix first 6 ingredients in bowl with 1/4 cup milk. Pour into 6 × 12-inch baking dish. Combine biscuit mix and 2/3 cup milk in bowl. Roll out 1/8-inch thick on floured surface. Sprinkle with cheese. Roll as for jelly roll. Cut into 1-inch slices. Arrange over salmon mixture. Bake at 375 degrees for 30 minutes or until biscuits are golden brown. Yield: 6 servings.

Laura Hill
Spartanburg, South Carolina

Rice and Salmon Casserole

2 tbsp. butter, melted
2 tbsp. flour
1 c. pureed tomatoes
1 tsp. sugar
1 1/4 tsp. salt
Dash of cloves and pepper
1/2 c. rice, cooked
1 can salmon, drained
1 sm. onion, chopped

Melt butter in saucepan. Add flour, blending well. Stir in tomatoes and seasonings. Cook until thick, stirring constantly. Add rice; mix well. Place in greased casserole. Combine salmon and onion in bowl; mix well. Spoon over rice mixture. Bake at 350 degrees for 1/2 hour.

JoAnn Bartek
Wilber, Nebraska

Salmon Cassolette

1 1-lb. can salmon
Milk
1 tbsp. chopped green pepper
1 clove of garlic, chopped
1/3 c. melted butter
1/3 c. flour
2 tsp. dry mustard
1/4 tsp. pepper
1 c. grated cheese
1 c. macaroni, cooked
1/4 c. chopped pimento

Drain salmon, reserving liquid. Add enough milk to measure 2 cups liquid. Saute green pepper with garlic in saucepan until tender. Add flour, mustard and pepper, blending well. Add liquid gradually; cook until thick, stirring constantly. Stir in cheese until melted. Layer macaroni, salmon and sauce in buttered baking dish. Bake at 350 degrees for 25 minutes. Garnish with additional cheese and pimento.

Delores S. Barber
Laurinburg, North Carolina

Salmon-Mushroom Souffle

1 can cream of celery soup
6 eggs, separated
1 8-oz. can sliced mushrooms, drained
1 1-lb. can pink salmon, drained, flaked

Heat soup in saucepan over low heat until simmering, stirring frequently. Beat egg yolks until thick. Stir a small amount of soup into egg yolks. Stir egg yolks into soup. Beat egg whites until stiff peaks form. Fold into soup mixture. Fold in mushrooms, blending well. Place salmon in 2-quart casserole. Pour mushroom mixture over top. Bake at 350 degrees for 1 hour. Serve immediately. Yield: 6 servings.

Ruth Robare
Albany, Oregon

Salmon-Potato Pie

1 lg. can salmon, drained, flaked
4 med. potatoes, boiled, drained
3 tbsp. margarine
1¼ c. milk
2 tbsp. flour

Spread salmon in casserole. Whip potatoes with 1 tablespoon margarine and ¼ cup milk. Melt remaining margarine in saucepan; blend in flour. Add remaining milk; cook until thick, stirring constantly. Pour over salmon. Spread potatoes over sauce. Bake at 400 degrees for 15 minutes or until bubbly.

Alice Blakeney
Runge, Texas

Salmon Steaks with Creamed Macaroni

4 1-inch thick salmon steaks
¼ c. melted butter
1 tbsp. salt
2 c. elbow macaroni
1 10-½ oz. can condensed cream of
    celery soup
½ c. milk
1 tbsp. lemon juice
¼ c. slivered ripe olives
1 tsp. instant minced onion

Place salmon steaks in butter in large shallow baking dish. Bake at 425 degrees for 20 minutes, brushing frequently with butter. Add salt to 3 quarts rapidly boiling water. Add macaroni gradually so that water continues to boil. Cook until tender, stirring occasionally; drain. Combine with remaining ingredients; spoon around salmon. Reduce temperature to 350 degrees. Bake for 15 minutes or until bubbly. Brush salmon with additional butter, as needed. Garnish with additional slivered olives, lemon slice or parsley. Yield: 4 servings.

Picture for this recipe on page 53.

Salmon Turbot

3 tbsp. butter
3 tbsp. flour
2 c. milk
3 eggs, beaten
2 tbsp. lemon juice
Seasonings to taste
1 1-lb. can salmon, flaked
½ c. buttered crumbs

Melt butter in saucepan; blend in flour. Add milk gradually. Cook until thickened, stirring constantly. Add eggs, lemon juice and seasonings; blend well. Layer sauce and salmon in greased casserole. Cover with buttered crumbs. Bake at 350 degrees for 45 minutes or until knife inserted in center comes out clean. Yield: 6 servings.

Cynthia Ebert
Ripon, Wisconsin

Chopstick Tuna

1 c. chopped celery
¼ c. finely chopped onion
2 tbsp. chopped green pepper
1 tbsp. butter
1 can cream of mushroom soup
¼ c. milk
1 3-oz. can chow mein noodles
1 4-oz. package salted cashews
1 7-oz. can tuna
⅛ tsp. pepper

Saute celery, onion and green pepper in butter in skillet until tender-crisp. Mix soup, milk and ¼ cup water in bowl. Reserve ½ cup noodles. Combine remaining noodles with vegetables, soup, tuna, nuts and pepper. Place in buttered 1½-quart baking dish. Sprinkle with reserved noodles. Bake at 350 degrees for 30 minutes. Yield: 3-4 servings.

Mary Amussen
Anna, Illinois

Doris's Tuna Casserole

1 c. macaroni
1 can cream of mushroom soup
1 family-sized can tuna, drained, flaked
1 c. peas
4 oz. sharp chesse, grated
1 c. crushed potato chips

Cook macaroni using package directions; drain. Combine macaroni and soup in bowl; mix well. Layer macaroni mixture, tuna, and cheese in buttered casserole. Top with potato chips. Bake at 350 degrees until heated through.

Doris R. Hahn
Des Moines, Iowa

Midwest Tuna Casserole

1 4-oz. package macaroni, cooked
1 10-oz. package frozen peas, cooked, drained
1 can celery soup
¼ c. milk
1 7½-oz. can tuna, drained, flaked
¼ c. Parmesan cheese
1 tbsp. onion, minced
½ c. salad dressing

Combine all ingredients in bowl; mix well. Pour into buttered 1½-quart casserole. Bake at 350 degrees for 25 minutes. Yield: 6 servings.

Joie Taylor
Menlo, Iowa

Quick Tuna Casserole

1 14-oz. package macaroni and cheese dinner
1 sm. onion, minced
1 can cream of mushroom soup
½ c. milk
1 6½-oz. can tuna
Butter
Crushed potato chips
2 slices American cheese, cut into ½-in. strips

Prepare macaroni and cheese dinner using package directions. Add next 4 ingredients; mix well. Coat buttered casserole with potato chips; add tuna mixture. Top with potato chips and cheese strips. Bake at 350 degrees for 20 minutes. Yield: 6-8 servings.

Lorene L. Arent
Wausa, Nebraska

Perfect Tuna

1 can cream of vegetable soup
⅓ to ½ c. milk
1 7-oz. can tuna, drained, flaked
2 hard-boiled eggs, sliced (opt.)
1 c. cooked peas
1 c. crushed potato chips

Blend soup and milk in 1-quart casserole. Stir in tuna, eggs and peas. Top with potato chips. Bake at 350 degrees for 30 minutes. Yield: 6 servings.

Betty Lou Horton
Tanner, Alabama

Scalloped Tuna

1 c. medium white sauce
1 tbsp. pimento
1 tbsp. chopped green pepper
1 c. bread crumbs
2 tbsp. butter
1 can tuna, drained, flaked

Combine white sauce, pimento and green pepper in bowl; mix well. Toss bread crumbs in bowl with butter. Layer tuna and bread crumbs in greased casserole. Add white sauce; top with bread crumbs. Bake at 375 degrees for ½ hour.

Delores Hickenbottom
Bloomfield, Nebraska

Tuna-Broccoli Casserole

1 pkg. frozen broccoli spears
1 can cream of celery soup
½ c. milk
1 7-oz. can tuna, drained, flaked
1¼ c. crushed potato chips

Cook broccoli using package directions until just tender; drain. Pour soup into greased 1-quart casserole. Add milk, stirring until blended. Add tuna. Arrange broccoli spears over tuna mixture. Sprinkle potato chips over top. Bake at 350 degrees for 20 minutes or until bubbly. Yield: 3-4 servings.

Dorothy S. Mitchell
Waterford, Connecticut

Tuna-Cheese Puff

3 eggs, separated
¾ c. milk
2 cans tuna, drained
1 c. soft bread crumbs
1 c. shredded Cheddar cheese
1 tsp. instant minced onion
½ tsp. salt
⅛ tsp. pepper
2 tsp. lemon juice
Parsley Sauce

Beat egg yolks with milk in bowl. Add tuna and remaining ingredients except egg whites; mix lightly. Beat egg whites until stiff but not dry; fold into tuna mixture. Turn into shallow 1-quart baking dish. Bake at 350 degrees for 30 minutes or until knife inserted in center comes out clean. Serve with Parsley Sauce.

Parsley Sauce

3 tbsp. butter
3 tbsp. flour
¾ tsp. salt
1½ c. milk
1 tbsp. lemon juice
1½ tbsp. chopped parsley

Melt butter in saucepan; stir in flour and salt. Stir in milk gradually. Cook over medium heat, stirring constantly, until thickened. Stir in lemon juice and parsley just before serving; serve over tuna.

Agnes Huffman
Modesto, California

Tuna Moussaka

1 med. eggplant, pared, sliced
⅓ c. chopped onion
3 tbsp. dry white wine
2 tbsp. cornstarch
2 c. skimmed milk
½ tsp. salt
⅛ tsp. pepper
¼ tsp. cinnamon
Dash of nutmeg
1 7-oz. can tuna, drained
2 eggs, beaten
1 c. cottage cheese
½ c. grated Parmesan cheese

Cook eggplant in boiling water to cover in saucepan for 3 or 4 minutes. Drain on paper towels. Place onion and wine in medium saucepan; cover. Cook over moderate heat for 5 minutes. Mix cornstarch with ¼ cup milk; stir until smooth. Add to saucepan with remaining milk, salt, pepper, cinnamon and nutmeg. Bring to a boil, stirring constantly. Remove from heat. Mix tuna with ½ cup onion sauce. Combine eggs, cottage cheese and remaining onion sauce; mix well. Place half the eggplant slices in bottom of 8 × 8 × 2-inch baking dish. Cover with tuna mixture. Sprinkle with ¼ cup Parmesan cheese. Add remaining eggplant slices. Pour cottage cheese mixture over all. Sprinkle with remaining ¼ cup cheese. Bake at 350 degrees for 50 to 55 minutes, or until custard topping is set. Let stand for 10 minutes before cutting into squares. Yield: 6 servings.

Picture for this recipe on cover.

Tuna-Noodle Bake

1 8-oz. package med. noodles, cooked
2 cans cream of mushroom soup
1 c. grated Cheddar cheese
½ tsp. Worcestershire sauce
2 cans tuna, drained, flaked
½ c. fine cracker crumbs
2 tbsp. butter
3 hard-boiled eggs, sliced

Heat soup and 1 cup water in saucepan over medium heat. Add cheese and Worcestershire sauce. Stir until smooth; remove from heat. Add tuna and noodles; blend well. Pour into greased 1½-quart casserole. Sprinkle with cracker crumbs; dot with butter. Top with eggs. Bake at 350 degrees for 40 to 50 minutes. Yield: 8 servings.

Anna Brandon
Fort Worth, Texas

Tuna Potpie

1 c. drained canned peas
1 can chunk-style tuna
1½ c. diced carrots
1½ c. diced potatoes
3 tbsp. chopped onion
Milk
¼ c. flour
¼ c. butter, melted
Seasonings to taste
1 unbaked pie crust

Drain peas, reserving liquid in saucepan. Add carrots, potatoes and onion. Cook until tender-crisp; drain, reserving liquid. Drain tuna, reserving liquid. Add enough milk to the two reserved liquids to measure 2 cups. Blend flour into butter in saucepan; add liquid gradually. Cook until thickened, stirring constantly. Add tuna, vegetables and seasonings; toss gently. Place in greased 1½-quart casserole; cover with pie crust. Bake at 425 degrees until crust is brown. Yield: 6 servings.

Nancy H. Tyrrell
Carleton, Michigan

Tuna Ramekins Chasseur

¼ lb. mushrooms, sliced
¼ c. chopped onion
¼ c. dry vermouth
2 7 oz. cans tuna, drained
3 eggs
1½ c. buttermilk
¼ tsp. salt
½ tsp. basil
¼ c. chopped parsley
¾ c. grated Parmesan cheese
1 lg. tomato, peeled, cut into 6 slices

Cook mushrooms and onion in vermouth in small covered saucepan, over medium heat for 5 minutes. Uncover. Cook until vermouth evaporates. Layer tuna with mushroom mixture in 6 individual ramekins. Beat eggs with buttermilk, salt, basil, parsley and ½ cup cheese in bowl. Pour over tuna and mushrooms. Top each ramekin with tomato slice. Sprinkle with remaining ¼ cup cheese. Bake at 325 degrees for 20 to 25 minutes or until set. Yield: 6 servings.

Picture for this recipe on cover.

Tuna-Stuffed Cabbage Rolls

12 lg. cabbage leaves
2 7-oz. cans tuna, drained, flaked
1 c. cooked rice
1 c. finely chopped celery with leaves
½ c. finely chopped onion
¼ c. chopped parsley
1 egg, slightly beaten
1 tbsp. Dijon-style mustard
2 tsp. caraway seed. (opt.)
½ tsp. salt
2 tsp. lemon juice
4 chicken bouillon cubes
½ c. buttermilk
1 tbsp. cornstarch
¼ tsp. nutmeg
⅛ tsp. pepper
2 tbsp. prepared horseradish
1 tsp. sugar

Cook cabbage leaves in boiling water to cover in large saucepan for 2 minutes. Drain well. Cut lengthwise about 2 inches through heavy vein of each leaf. Place tuna in large bowl. Add rice, celery, onion, parsley, egg, mustard, caraway seed, ¼ teaspoon salt and lemon juice; mix well. Place ¼ cup of mixture on each cabbage leaf. Roll up, tucking in ends securely; fasten with toothpicks. Place rolls in large skillet with 3 cups water and chicken bouillon cubes; cover. Simmer for 15 to 20 minutes or until rolls are tender. Remove rolls to warm serving platter; cover. Reserve liquid. Mix buttermilk with cornstarch in small bowl until smooth. Stir into hot liquid in skillet gradually. Add remaining ¼ teaspoon salt, nutmeg, pepper, horseradish and sugar. Bring to a boil, stirring constantly. Simmer for 2 or 3 minutes. Pour sauce over cabbage rolls. Yield: 6 servings.

Picture for this recipe on cover.

Tuna-Vegetable Supper

1 med. cauliflower
1 c. sliced carrots
2 tbsp. chopped onion
1 tbsp. butter
1 can cream of mushroom soup
2 tbsp. milk
1 7-oz. can tuna, drained, flaked
Dash of nutmeg
½ c. cracker crumbs

Separate cauliflower into flowerets. Cook with carrots in boiling salted water in saucepan until tender-crisp. Drain. Place in 1½-quart casserole. Saute onion in butter in skillet until tender. Add onion, soup, milk, tuna and nutmeg; mix well. Pour over carrots. Sprinkle with crumbs. Bake at 350 degrees for 40 minutes or until slightly browned. Yield: 4 servings.

Ruth Park
Bend, Oregon

Eggplant-Clam Casserole

1 lg. eggplant, peeled, diced
2 tbsp. lemon juice
½ tsp. salt
2 c. thick white sauce
1 can minced clams
1 c. cracker crumbs
Buttered crumbs

Place eggplant in saucepan with lemon juice, salt and enough water to cover. Cook until tender; drain. Add white sauce. Add clams and cracker crumbs; mix well. Place in buttered casserole; top with buttered crumbs. Bake in 325-degree oven for 40 minutes.

Mrs. H. B. Watson
Saint Edward, Nebraska

Scalloped Clam Casserole

1 c. cracker crumbs
2 c. milk
1 egg, slightly beaten
1 tsp. grated onion
⅛ tsp. pepper
1 can minced clams

Combine cracker crumbs and milk in bowl. Stir in remaining ingredients. Place in greased 1½-quart casserole. Bake for 30 to 40 minutes at 350 degrees. Yield: 4-6 servings.

Beverly Abbott
Lisbon Falls, Maine

Lobster En Casserole

4 tbsp. chopped onion
1 clove of garlic, minced
2 tbsp. butter
1 11-oz. can Cheddar cheese soup
2 3-oz. cans sliced mushrooms, drained
½ c. milk
4 tbsp. dry Sherry
2 tbsp. snipped parsley
3 c. lobster
1 c. frozen peas, cooked, drained
2 tbsp. buttered bread crumbs

Saute onion and garlic in butter in skillet until tender. Stir in soup and mushrooms. Blend in milk, Sherry and parsley. Add lobster and peas. Cook until heated through, stirring constantly. Spoon into 4 one cup casseroles. Top with crumbs. Bake at 350 degrees for 25 to 30 minutes. Yield: 4 servings.

Marilyn Berousek
Maysville, Oklahoma

Lobster Supreme

12 oz. lobster
1 can cream of celery soup
1 can tomato soup
2 tbsp. Sherry
1 tbsp. lemon juice
Salt and pepper to taste
¼ c. bread crumbs
2 tbsp. butter

Combine lobster, soups, Sherry, lemon juice and seasonings in bowl; mix well. Pour into well-buttered casserole. Top with bread crumbs; dot with butter. Bake at 400 degrees until browned. Yield: 4 servings.

Martha Dawson
Dover, Delaware

Franklin Village Oysters

1 qt. oysters, drained
1¼ c. cracker meal
2 tsp. chopped chives
½ tsp. salt
¼ tsp. pepper
1 tsp. lemon juice
¼ c. cooking Sherry
2 tbsp. chopped parsley
¾ stick butter
¼ c. slivered toasted almonds
¾ c. half and half

Place half the oysters in shallow buttered casserole. Sprinkle with half the cracker meal, chives, salt, pepper, lemon juice, Sherry and parsley. Dot with half the butter; repeat layers. Cover with almonds; pour half and half over top. Refrigerate for 1 hour. Bake at 325 degrees for 35 minutes. Yield: 8 servings.

Shirley S. Allen
Detroit, Michigan

Scalloped Corn and Oysters

1 1-lb. can cream-style corn
1 can oyster stew
1 c. milk
¼ c. chopped celery
1 egg, slightly beaten

1 tbsp. chopped pimento
1½ c. cracker crumbs
2 tbsp. melted butter

Combine first 6 ingredients with 1 cup cracker crumbs in bowl; mix well. Pour into greased casserole. Combine butter and remaining cracker crumbs. Sprinkle over corn mixture. Bake at 350 degrees for 45 minutes.

Marian Baker
Sycamore, Illinois

Scalloped Oysters

¾ c. dry bread crumbs
¾ c. cracker crumbs
½ tsp. salt
¼ tsp. pepper
¼ tsp. celery salt
2 tbsp. chopped parsley
½ c. butter, melted
1 pt. oysters, drained
¼ tsp. Worcestershire sauce
1 c. milk

Combine first 7 ingredients in bowl; mix well. Alternate layers of crumb mixture and oysters in well-greased baking dish until all ingredients are used. Mix Worcestershire sauce and milk; pour over oysters. Bake at 400 degrees for 20 to 25 minutes or until brown.

Ruth Ann Jackson
Sellersburg, Indiana

Wild Rice and Oysters

¼ lb. butter, melted
2 c. wild rice, cooked, drained
2 pt. oysters
Salt, pepper and hot pepper sauce to
   taste
1 can cream of mushroom soup
1 c. light cream
1½ tsp. onion powder
¾ tsp. thyme
1½ tsp. curry powder
½ c. finely minced parsley

Combine butter and rice. Place half the rice in 9 × 13-inch baking dish. Cover with oysters. Season with salt, pepper and hot pepper sauce. Top with remaining rice. Mix next 5 ingredients in bowl. Pour over rice mixture. Bake at 325 degrees for 45 minutes. Garnish with parsley.

Ronnie Raney
Clarksdale, Mississippi

Alaska King Crab Souffle

1 c. chopped green onions
⅔ c. butter
½ c. flour
2 tsp. salt
1 tsp. pepper
1¼ c. light cream
⅓ c. tomato paste
8 eggs, separated
12 oz. crab meat, flaked

Saute onions in butter in skillet until tender. Stir in flour, salt and pepper. Cook over low heat until smooth, stirring constantly. Stir in cream and tomato paste. Bring to boiling point; stir in beaten egg yolks. Remove from heat; stir in crab meat. Cool to room temperature. Beat egg whites until stiff. Fold ¼ of the egg whites into crab meat mixture. Fold in remaining egg whites gently. Place in 2 buttered casseroles. Bake in 375-degree oven for 30 minutes or until knife inserted in center comes out clean. Garnish with parsley and lemon wedges. Serve immediately.

Helen Giles
Seldovia, Alaska

Crab Au Gratin

1 sm. onion, diced
4 tbsp. butter
2 tbsp. (rounded) flour
1½ c. milk
2 cans crab meat
1 sm. can pimento, diced
Salt and pepper to taste
1 c. grated sharp cheese
Buttered bread crumbs

Saute onion in butter in skillet until soft. Blend in flour; add milk. Cook until thickened, stirring constantly. Add crab meat, pimento, salt, pepper and cheese. Place half the mixture in greased casserole. Cover with bread crumbs. Add remaining crab mixture; top with bread crumbs. Bake in 350-degree oven for 20 minutes. Yield: 6 servings.

Caroline J. Ebell
Baker, Oregon

Elizabeth's Crab Meat Casserole

2 tbsp. butter
2 tbsp. flour
1 c. milk
½ c. grated Cheddar cheese
½ tsp. salt
Few grains of pepper
1 lb. crab meat
1 can cream of mushroom soup
Buttered bread crumbs

Melt butter in saucepan; blend in flour. Stir in milk. Cook over low heat until thick, stirring constantly. Stir in cheese until melted; season to taste. Place crab meat in buttered 1-quart casserole. Cover with soup and cheese sauce. Sprinkle with crumbs. Bake at 350 degrees for 45 minutes. Yield: 4 servings.

Elizabeth Miner
Pawcatuck, Connecticut

Crab Quiche Lorraine

4 oz. crab meat
2 eggs
1 c. evaporated skim milk
2 oz. Swiss cheese, grated
Dash of pepper
½ tsp. each salt, nutmeg

Spread crab meat in 1-quart casserole. Beat eggs with milk in bowl. Add grated cheese and seasonings; mix well. Pour cheese mixture over crab meat. Bake at 375 degrees for 30 minutes.

Valery V. Laing
Bossier City, Louisiana

Patricia's Crab Meat Casserole

½ c. cooking Sherry
2 c. medium white sauce
1 lb. crab meat
Grated sharp cheese

Blend Sherry into white sauce. Alternate layers of crab meat and sauce in casserole. Top with cheese. Bake at 350 degrees until bubbly.

Patricia Baldy
North Wildwood, New Jersey

New England Seafood Casserole

⅓ c. butter
3 tbsp. flour
1 tsp. salt

Dash of pepper
2 c. milk
½ c. shredded cheese
¼ c. sliced onion
1 c. sour cream
1 c. large curd cottage cheese
1 6-oz. package wide noodles, cooked
1 can crab meat
¼ c. corn flake crumbs

Melt 3 tablespoons butter in saucepan. Blend in flour, salt and pepper. Stir in milk. Cook until thick, stirring constantly. Blend in ¼ cup cheese with next 4 ingredients. Layer crab meat and noodles in 2-quart casserole. Melt remaining butter. Toss with crumbs and remaining cheese. Spoon around edge of casserole. Bake at 350 degrees for 40 to 50 minutes or until bubbly. Yield: 10 servings.

Gertrude Wagner
Concord, Vermont

Chinese Casserole

1 lg. can chow mein noodles
1 can cream of mushroom soup
1 c. finely chopped celery
1 lg. can shrimp

Combine all ingredients in bowl with ½ cup water; mix well. Place in shallow casserole. Bake at 350 degrees for 30 minutes. Yield: 4 servings.

Madeline Johnson
Pinehurst, Idaho

Deviled Eggs and Shrimp

12 med. hard-boiled eggs
1 tbsp. parsley flakes
2 tbsp. mayonnaise
2 tsp. lemon juice
⅛ tsp. garlic powder
⅛ tsp. curry powder
2 tbsp. melted butter
3 tbsp. flour
2 tsp. prepared mustard
¾ c. milk
Salt and pepper to taste
1 lb. frozen cooked shrimp, thawed

Cut eggs in half lengthwise; remove yolks. Mash egg yolks in bowl; add next 8 ingredients. Mix well. Add milk, salt and pepper; mix until smooth. Place egg whites, cavity side up, in single layer in greased, 10-inch square casserole. Place 1 shrimp in each egg, spread remaining shrimp around eggs. Spoon egg yolk mixture over top. Bake, covered, at 350 degrees for ½ hour. Yield: 12 servings.

Cora E. Fagre
Lafayette, Colorado

Florence's Seafood Casserole

1 sm. onion, minced
¼ c. butter
3 tbsp. flour
1½ tsp. salt
½ tsp. mustard
¼ tsp. pepper
3 c. milk
4 c. sharp grated cheese
½ c. Sherry
6 c. cooked chopped shrimp
¼ c. lemon juice
1 lb. small shell macaroni, cooked
1 c. crushed saltine crackers

Saute onion in butter in saucepan. Blend in flour, salt, mustard and pepper. Add milk. Cook until thick, stirring constantly. Add 3 cups cheese, stirring until cheese is melted. Add Sherry. Sprinkle shrimp with lemon juice. Alternate layers of macaroni, shrimp and cheese sauce in buttered casserole, ending with cheese sauce. Sprinkle with remaining cheese and cracker crumbs. Bake at 400 degrees for 35 minutes. Yield: 15 servings.

Florence D. Tolli
Plainville, Connecticut

Skillet Shrimp and Rice

½ clove of garlic, minced
1 c. diced celery
1 onion, chopped
1 bay leaf, crumbled
¼ c. oil
1 5-oz. package minute rice
1 chicken bouillon cube
¼ c. chopped stuffed olives (opt.)
⅛ tsp. thyme
1 tsp. salt
⅛ tsp. pepper
2 lb. shrimp, cooked

Saute garlic, celery and onion with bay leaf in oil in skillet until tender. Add rice. Cook until brown, stirring constantly. Dissolve bouillon cube in 1¾ cups boiling water. Add with remaining ingredients except shrimp to rice. Bring to a boil. Simmer, covered, for 10 minutes. Stir in shrimp. Cook until heated through. Garnish with sliced olives. Yield: 6 servings.

Picture for this recipe above.

New Orleans Shrimp Casserole

½ c. chopped green pepper
½ c. chopped onion
2 tbsp. butter
3 c. shrimp
1 tbsp. lemon juice
2 c. cooked rice
1 can tomato soup
¾ c. light cream
¼ c. cooking Sherry
¾ tsp. salt
¼ tsp. nutmeg
¼ c. toasted almonds

Saute green pepper and onion in butter in saucepan until tender; stir in remaining ingredients except almonds. Pour into 2-quart casserole. Bake at 350 degrees for 30 minutes or until bubbly. Top with almonds. Yield: 6-8 servings.

Nell P. Stevens
Indianola, Mississippi

Crab-Shrimp Imperial

1 vegetable bouillon cube
¾ c. rice, cooked
1 tbsp. cooked parsley
1 can frozen cream of shrimp soup
½ c. milk
1 tsp. lemon juice
⅛ tsp. nutmeg
1 7-oz. can King crab, drained
¾ lb. cooked cleaned shrimp
1 can sliced mushrooms
½ c. soft bread crumbs
¼ c. toasted slivered almonds
2 tbsp. melted butter

Dissolve bouillon cube in 1 cup hot water; pour over rice. Stir in parsley; set aside. Combine soup and milk in top of double boiler. Heat over simmering water until bubbly, stirring occasionally. Stir in lemon juice and nutmeg. Reserve 3 pieces crab meat and 3 shrimp for garnish. Fold remaining crab meat, shrimp and mushrooms into sauce. Alternate layers of sauce mixture and rice in buttered casserole. Toss last 3 ingredients together. Spoon around edge of casserole. Bake at 350 degrees for 35 to 45 minutes or until bubbly. Place reserved shrimp and crab in center.

Dorothy M. Hardin
Lebanon, Illinois

Crab and Shrimp Supreme

1 c. diced celery
¼ c. chopped onion
¼ c. chopped green pepper
2 tbsp. butter
1 c. cooked shrimp
2 c. flaked crab meat
2 tbsp. flour
½ tsp. salt
2 tbsp. Rhine wine
1 c. cottage cheese
½ c. sour cream

Saute celery, onion and green pepper in butter in skillet for 3 minutes. Blend shrimp, crab meat and flour; add to sauteed vegetables. Add salt and wine. Blend cottage cheese and sour cream; add to crab mixture. Pour into buttered casserole. Bake at 350 degrees for 35 minutes. Yield: 6 servings.

Mrs. Norman G. Johnston
Liverpool, New York

Eastern Shore Casserole Supreme

1 lb. back fin crab meat
1 lb. cooked shrimp
¼ c. soft bread crumbs
1 sm. onion, grated
1 tbsp. chopped chives
1 egg, beaten
¾ c. sour cream
1 can cream of mushroom soup
½ c. sliced mushrooms (opt.)
1 tbsp. horseradish
1 tsp. mustard
Buttered bread crumbs
Butter

Slice shrimp into halves. Combine all ingredients except bread crumbs and butter in bowl; mix well. Pour into greased casserole. Sprinkle with crumbs; dot with butter. Bake at 375 degrees until golden brown. Yield: 4-6 servings.

Virginia O. Savedge
Eastville, Virginia

Eggplant and Seafood

1 med. eggplant, peeled
1 med. onion, chopped
2 cloves of garlic, chopped
½ green pepper, chopped
Parsley
2 tbsp. bacon drippings
4 slices dry bread
1 lb. shrimp
1 lb. crab meat
Salt and pepper
Dash of red pepper (opt.)
Buttered bread crumbs

Boil eggplant in salted water in saucepan until tender; drain and slice. Saute onion, garlic, green pepper and parsley in bacon drippings in skillet. Remove from heat; add eggplant. Soak bread in water; squeeze out excess liquid. Add to eggplant mixture. Add seafood; season to taste; mix well. Place in well-greased casserole. Top with buttered bread crumbs. Bake at 350 degrees for 30 minutes. Yield: 6 servings.

Mrs. Brack Jones, Jr.
Liberty, Texas

Variety

Creamed Corned Beef Casserole

6 to 7 med. potatoes, peeled, diced
2 tbsp. minced onion
Salt
2 c. medium white sauce
1 can corned beef, flaked
Pepper to taste
⅓ c. buttered crumbs

Combine potatoes and onion with a small amount of salted water in saucepan. Boil until potatoes are just tender; drain. Combine with white sauce and corned beef. Season with salt and pepper. Place in buttered 2-quart casserole. Top with crumbs. Bake in 350-degree oven for 30 to 35 minutes or until golden brown. Yield: 6 servings.

Martha Ann Johnson
Manton, Michigan

Corned Beef and Macaroni

1 can cream of chicken soup
1 soup can milk
2 tbsp. onion flakes
8 slices American cheese
1 can corned beef, chopped
1 8-oz. package macaroni, cooked
Buttered bread crumbs

Combine soup, milk, and onion flakes in large saucepan. Add cheese. Cook over medium heat stirring constantly until cheese melts. Stir in corned beef and macaroni. Pour into 2-quart casserole. Top with crumbs. Bake at 350 degrees for 30 minutes or until brown.

Mary J. Strand
Jamestown, New York

Corny Noodle Casserole

4 c. cooked egg noodles
1 can corned beef, chopped
1 lb. Cheddar cheese, shredded
1 can cream of mushroom soup
1 c. milk

Alternate layers of noodles, corned beef and cheese in buttered 2-quart casserole. Dilute soup with milk; pour over top. Bake at 350 degrees for 45 minutes to 1 hour. Yield: 6 servings.

Alice M. Carlisle
Brimley, Michigan

Corned Beef and Noodle Casserole

1 8-oz. package noodles, cooked
1 can corned beef
1 can mushroom soup
1 sm. can peas
1 sm. onion, chopped
Buttered crumbs

Alternate layers of noodles, corned beef, soup, peas and onions in casserole until all ingredients are used. Top with crumbs. Bake at 350 degrees for 45 minutes.

Elenor Rollins
Ft. Myers, Florida

Ruth's Corned Beef Dinner

1 med. onion, chopped
1 green pepper, diced
2 tbsp. bacon drippings
1 can corned beef, flaked
1 can mushroom soup
Wide noodles, cooked
½ c. bread crumbs
2 tbsp. butter

Saute onion and green pepper in bacon drippings in skillet. Add corned beef and soup; mix well. Alternate layers of corned beef mixture and noodles in casserole until all ingredients are used, ending with corned beef. Top with crumbs; dot with butter. Bake at 350 degrees for 45 minutes or until brown. Yield: 6 servings.

Ruth Fanelli
Riverview, Florida

Corned Beef-Vegetable Casserole

1 can corned beef, flaked
1 med. onion, chopped
1 can green beans, drained
5 to 6 med. potatoes, cooked, sliced
1 can cream of celery soup
2 tbsp. milk

Combine first 3 ingredients in bowl; toss to mix. Alternate layers of potatoes and corned beef mixture in greased casserole until all ingredients are used ending with corned beef. Blend soup with milk; pour over top. Bake at 350 degrees for 20 to 30 minutes.

Anne M. Thurbide
Bras d'or, Nova Scotia, Canada

Reuben Casserole

1 12-oz. can corned beef
¼ c. Thousand Island dressing
1 1-lb. can sauerkraut, drained
½ lb. Swiss cheese, shredded
¼ c. margarine, melted
6 slices rye bread, crumbled

Crumble corned beef into well-greased 12 ×
8-inch baking dish. Dot with Thousand Island
dressing. Spread sauerkraut over top. Cover
with cheese. Toss bread crumbs with margarine. Sprinkle over casserole. Bake in 350-
degree oven for 30 minutes or until hot and
bubbly.

Carolyn K. Simpson
Burbank, California

Yankee Red Flannel Hash

1½ c. finely chopped cooked corned beef
3 c. finely chopped cooked potatoes
1½ c. finely chopped cooked beets
⅓ c. finely chopped onion
⅓ c. milk
1 tsp. salt
Hot sauce to taste
3 tbsp. shortening
1 can French-fried onion rings

Combine corned beef, potatoes, beets and
onion in bowl; mix in milk. Add salt and hot
sauce; mix well. Melt shortening in skillet.
Spread beef mixture evenly over bottom of
skillet. Cook over medium heat until underside
is brown and crusty. Top with onion rings. Bake
at 275 degrees for 20 minutes. Yield: 4
servings.

June Kreutzkampf
Maquoketa, Iowa

Creamy Beef-Macaroni Casserole

2 tbsp., each chopped onion, green
    pepper
2 tbsp. butter
2½ oz. dried beef, cut up
1 can cream of chicken soup
¾ can milk
¼ tsp. pepper
1¼ c. macaroni
½ c. shredded cheese

Saute onion and green pepper in butter in
skillet. Add dried beef. Cook until browned.
Stir in soup, milk and pepper. Cook macaroni
according to package directions, using unsalt-
ed water; drain. Add to dried beef mixture.
Pour into 1½-quart casserole. Sprinkle with
cheese. Bake for 20 to 30 minutes at 350
degrees. Yield: 6-8 servings.

Mrs. Merle Twesme
Arcadia, Wisconsin

Crunchy Beef-Noodle Casserole

¼ lb. dried beef, shredded
1 pkg. frozen peas
½ c. diced celery
1 can cream of chicken soup
½ c. milk
¼ tsp. each garlic salt, pepper
1 5-oz. can chow mein noodles

Cover dried beef with boiling water; drain.
Separate frozen peas under running water.
Combine all ingredients except noodles in
bowl. Alternate layers of noodles and dried
beef mixture in 1½-quart casserole, beginning
and ending with noodles. Bake in 375-degree
oven for 30 minutes. Yield: 4 servings.

Lucille Johnston
Litchfield, Illinois

Dried Beef and Macaroni Bake

¼ c. each chopped onion, celery
¼ lb. dried beef, shredded
¼ c. oil
¼ c. flour
2 c. milk
2 c. cooked macaroni
½ tsp. each salt, pepper
1 tbsp. minced parsley
⅓ c. grated American cheese

Saute onion, celery and dried beef in hot oil in
skillet until onion is golden. Stir in flour. Add
milk gradually. Cook until slightly thickened,
stirring constantly. Add macaroni, seasonings
and parsley. Pour into greased 1½-quart
casserole. Sprinkle with cheese. Bake in 350-
degree oven for 15 minutes. Yield: 6 servings.

Mrs. Garry C. Pittman
Darien, Georgia

Dried Beef-Broccoli Casserole

8 tbsp. margarine, melted
6 tbsp. flour
4 c. milk
2 lb. fresh broccoli, cooked
1 tsp. salt
½ tsp. pepper
½ lb. dried beef, chopped
1 tsp. Worcestershire sauce
1 8-oz. package noodles, cooked
1 c. bread crumbs

Blend 4 tablespoons margarine and flour in saucepan; stir in milk. Cook over low heat until thick, stirring constantly. Chop broccoli coarsely. Add broccoli and next 4 ingredients to sauce; mix well. Spread noodles in greased 3-quart casserole. Spoon sauce over top, toss lightly to mix. Mix bread crumbs with remaining margarine. Sprinkle over casserole. Bake at 375 degrees for 20 minutes. Yield: 6-8 servings.

Jaci Courte
New Lebanon, Ohio

Cheesy Potato-Frank Casserole

1 egg, beaten
1 tbsp. chopped parsley
½ tsp. salt
⅛ tsp. pepper
2 c. hot mashed potatoes
¼ lb. pimento cheese, sliced
½ lb. frankfurters, scored
1 sm. onion, sliced, rings separated
2 tbsp. melted margarine

Stir egg, parsley, salt and pepper into potatoes; beat well. Place in greased 1-quart baking dish. Make depression in center; build potatoes up around sides of dish with back of spoon. Place cheese slices in depression. Place frankfurters over cheese. Top with onion. Brush with margarine. Bake in 375-degree oven for 30 minutes or until lightly browned.

June W. Bostick
Federalsburg, Maryland

Frankly Vegetable Pie

1 10-oz. package frozen mixed
vegetables, cooked, drained
½ lb. frankfurters
2 tbsp. melted butter
1 8-oz. package corn bread mix

Slice frankfurters ½ inch thick. Spread in casserole. Combine vegetables and butter. Pour over frankfurters. Prepare corn bread using package directions. Spread over vegetables. Bake at 375 degrees for 20 minutes. Yield: 6-8 servings.

Karen A. Boytz
Bellevue, Washington

Glazed Frankfurter Casserole

2 1-lb. cans pork and beans with tomato
sauce
6 frankfurters
2 tbsp. brown sugar
1 tsp. prepared mustard
1 tsp. Worcestershire sauce

Pour beans into shallow baking dish. Slash skin of frankfurters. Arrange on beans, cut side up. Combine brown sugar, mustard and Worcestershire sauce in bowl. Spread over frankfurters. Bake at 450 degrees for 20 minutes or until frankfurters are browned. Yield: 4 servings.

Mildred Wood
Gaffney, South Carolina

Kraut-Frankfurter Lasagna

4 c. sauerkraut, well-drained
1 lb. frankfurters, sliced thin
1 12-oz. package American cheese slices
½ c. finely chopped onion
½ c. finely chopped parsley
8 tbsp. butter
1 16-oz. carton creamed cottage cheese
1 egg, beaten
1 tsp. caraway seed
6 tbsp. flour
1 tsp. salt
Dash of cayenne pepper
2¾ c. milk
9 lasagna noodles, cooked

Reserve ¼ cup sauerkraut, 2 frankfurters and 2 slices cheese for garnish. Saute onion and parsley in 2 tablespoons butter in skillet until tender. Stir in sauerkraut, frankfurters, cottage cheese, egg and caraway seed; mix well. Set aside. Melt remaining butter in saucepan; blend in flour, salt and cayenne pepper. Add milk. Cook until thick, stirring constantly. Stir in remaining cheese cut in strips until cheese melts. Alternate layers of lasagna noodles, frankfurter mixture and cheese sauce in 3-quart baking dish until all ingredients are used, ending with cheese sauce. Bake, covered, at 375 degrees for 30 minutes; uncover. Garnish with reserved ingredients as pictured. Bake for 15 minutes longer. Let stand for 5 minutes before cutting. Yield: 8 servings.

Picture for this recipe on page 65.

Hot Potatoes and Franks

½ lb. frankfurters
1 tbsp. butter
½ env. onion soup mix
1 tbsp. flour
1 tbsp. sugar
Dash of pepper
2 tbsp. vinegar
4 c. sliced cooked potatoes
½ c. sour cream

Brown frankfurters in butter in skillet. Remove from skillet. Stir soup mix, flour, sugar and pepper into pan drippings. Add ½ cup water and vinegar; stir well. Add frankfurters. Bring to a boil, stirring constantly. Reduce heat; cover. Simmer for 10 minutes. Add potatoes and sour cream. Heat just to boiling point.

Martha Harless
Virginia Beach, Virginia

Wiener-Bean Casserole

2 1-lb. can pork and beans
1 env. dry onion soup mix
⅓ c. catsup
2 tbsp. brown sugar
1 tbsp. prepared mustard
1 lb. frankfurters, sliced

Combine all ingredients with ¼ cup water in 2-quart casserole. Bake at 350 degrees for 1 hour. Yield: 6-8 servings.

Mary Westman
Denver, Colorado

Wiener-Macaroni Casserole

1 c. shell macaroni
1 lb. wieners, chopped
1½ c. mixed vegetables
1 can cream of chicken soup
½ tsp. each salt, pepper, sugar
1 tsp. oregano
1 can onion rings

Cook macaroni in 2 cups salted water for 8 minutes; drain. Arrange layers of macaroni, wieners, vegetables and soup in casserole. Sprinkle with salt, pepper, sugar and oregano. Place onion rings on top. Bake, covered, at 325 degrees for 40 minutes. Yield: 4 servings.

Jency Ree Henderson
Clinton, Mississippi

Dove and Rice Casserole

15 dove
Oil
1 med. onion, chopped
2 cloves of garlic, finely chopped
1 tsp. lemon-pepper seasoning
1 c. rice
1 sm. can mushrooms
1 bouillon cube
Juice of 2 lemons
½ c. cooking Sherry
Salt and pepper to taste

Brown dove in a small amount of oil in skillet. Set aside. Saute onion in oil in skillet. Add remaining ingredients with 1 cup water; mix well. Spoon into large baking dish. Arrange dove over rice mixture. Bake at 350 degrees for 1 hour.

Madeline Merrill
Houston, Texas

Quail on the Green

½ c. margarine
8 to 12 quail
Salt and pepper to taste
Garlic salt to taste
2 c. sour cream
2 cans cream of asparagus soup
½ lb. fresh mushrooms, sliced
½ c. Sherry
Parmesan cheese
2 bunches fresh asparagus, cooked

Melt margarine in baking pan. Place quail in pan; sprinkle lightly with salt, pepper and garlic salt. Combine sour cream, soup, mushrooms and Sherry in bowl; mix well. Pour ¼ of the sauce over quail. Sprinkle generously with Parmesan cheese. Arrange asparagus over quail; pour remaining sauce over asparagus. Sprinkle with Parmesan cheese. Bake in 350-degree oven until tender.

Meta West
Abilene, Kansas

Venison-Stuffed Cabbage Leaves

2 lb. ground venison
5 tbsp. chopped onion
3 tbsp. butter
2 c. cooked rice
1 tbsp. chopped dill
Salt to taste
Pepper to taste
12 cabbage leaves
1 8-oz. can tomato sauce

Brown venison and onion in butter in skillet. Mix in rice, dill, salt and pepper. Place cabbage leaves in boiling water for 1 minute; drain. Dry on paper toweling. Place equal amount of meat mixture in center of each leaf. Fold leaf over; secure with toothpicks. Place filled leaves in greased baking dish. Pour tomato sauce over leaves. Bake in 325-degree oven for 45 minutes. Yield: 6 servings.

Eleanor Weatherhead
Dayton, Ohio

Armenian-Style Lamb

6 carrots, peeled
8 med. potatoes, peeled, cut into halves
1 eggplant, chopped
2 onions, sliced
1 lb. squash, sliced
1 28-oz. can tomatoes, drained
Several sprigs of parsley, chopped
1 bay leaf
1 clove of garlic, minced
2 tsp. salt
½ tsp. pepper
6 lamb chops
¼ c. flour

Arrange carrots, potatoes, eggplant, onions and squash in deep baking dish. Top with tomatoes. Combine parsley, bay leaf, half the garlic, 1½ teaspoons salt and ¼ teaspoon pepper; sprinkle over vegetables. Rub lamb chops with remaining garlic, salt and pepper. Arrange over vegetables. Bake, covered, in 375-degree oven for 1 hour. Mix flour with ½ cup water until smooth. Stir flour mixture into pan juices. Bake, uncovered, for 20 minutes longer, or until gravy is thickened. Yield: 6 servings.

Marie Heltzel
Lake Butler, Florida

Luceil's Lamb Casserole

2 med. onions, sliced
5 mushrooms, sliced
1 tbsp. bacon drippings
1½ c. cubed leg of lamb
2 med. boiled potatoes, cubed
½ tsp. salt
1 tsp. Worcestershire sauce
1 c. gravy

Saute onions and mushrooms in bacon drippings in skillet. Add remaining ingredients; mix well. Pour into greased baking dish. Bake at 350 degrees for 30 minutes. Yield: 4 servings.

Luceil Batton
Corsicana, Texas

Tourlou

2 onions, chopped
¼ c. butter
2 lb. lean lamb, cubed
Salt to taste
2 sm. zucchini, sliced
1 med. eggplant, peeled and cut into
    1-in. cubes
2 lg. green peppers, diced
1 can okra
1 1-lb. can cut green beans, drained
2 tbsp. Brandy
¼ c. dry white wine

Cook onions in butter in large skillet until lightly browned. Add lamb, salt and ½ cup water. Simmer until lamb is almost tender. Add 1 cup water, zucchini, eggplant and green peppers; cover tightly. Cook for 20 minutes or until vegetables are tender, adding hot water, if needed. Reduce heat; add okra and green beans. Simmer for 10 minutes. Stir in Brandy and wine. Heat to serving temperature. Yield: 6 servings.

Hazel C. Tassis
Imperial, California

Baked Liver and Onions

2 lg. onions, sliced
½ c. butter
½ c. dry red wine
¼ c. chopped parsley
1 bay leaf, crumbled
1 tsp. each thyme, salt

Pepper
6 slices beef liver
½ c. flour

Arrange onions in baking dish. Dot with butter. Add wine, parsley, bay leaf, thyme, salt, pepper and ½ cup water; cover. Bake at 350 degrees for 30 minutes. Coat liver with flour. Place over onion slices. Cover. Bake for 30 minutes, basting two or three times. Remove cover. Bake for 10 minutes longer. Yield: 6 servings.

Mrs. George Ballard
Harriman, Tennessee

Liver and Rice Creole

2 lb. liver
1 c. flour
¼ c. shortening
1 c. chopped onions
1 tbsp. salt
5 c. tomato puree
½ c. chopped green pepper
4 c. cooked rice
2 c. oven-toasted rice cereal
2 tbsp. melted margarine

Cut liver into ½-inch cubes. Coat with flour. Saute in shortening in skillet until browned. Add onions. Saute until brown. Add salt, tomato puree and green pepper. Simmer for 5 minutes. Alternate layers of rice and tomato mixture in 10 × 16-inch baking dish. Combine rice cereal and margarine in small bowl. Sprinkle over liver. Bake at 325 degrees for about 30 minutes. Yield: 20 servings.

LeNora Hudson
Sulphur, Oklahoma

Smothered Liver Casserole

1 lb. beef liver, sliced
¼ c. flour
¼ c. shortening
3 med. onions, chopped
¼ c. chopped celery
1 c. canned tomatoes
1 tsp. salt
⅛ tsp. pepper

Roll each piece of liver in flour. Brown lightly on both sides in hot shortening in skillet. Place in casserole. Brown onions in same skillet. Add

celery and tomatoes. Simmer until heated through. Spoon vegetables over liver. Season with salt and pepper. Cover. Bake at 350 degrees for 45 minutes. Yield: 6 servings.

Dorothy West
Littlefield, Texas

Chicken Livers Baked with Rice

¾ lb. chicken livers
Salt and pepper to taste
Flour
4 tbsp. butter
3 tbsp. each finely chopped celery, onion
1 c. rice
2 c. chicken broth
1 tsp. minced parsley

Sprinkle livers with salt and pepper. Shake in small amount of flour in paper bag. Brown in butter in skillet. Place in 6-cup casserole. Saute celery, onion, and rice in butter remaining in skillet until lightly browned. Add broth; stir well. Add parsley; pour over livers. Cover. Bake at 350 degrees for 30 minutes or until rice is tender and liquid is absorbed. Yield: 6 servings.

Imogene Brashear
Palatka, Florida

Pantry-Shelf Special

1 sm. can sweet potatoes, sliced
1 12-oz. can luncheon meat
4 canned pineapple slices
Pineapple syrup
¼ c. packed brown sugar
1 tbsp. cornstarch
¼ tsp. salt
¼ c. cooking Sherry
2 tbsp. butter

Arrange sweet potatoes in 6 × 10-inch baking dish. Cut luncheon meat into 4 slices. Layer over potatoes; top with pineapple. Blend syrup, sugar and cornstarch in saucepan. Cook until thick and clear, stirring constantly. Stir in remaining ingredients. Pour over pineapple. Bake at 375 degrees for 40 minutes. Yield: 4 servings.

Yvonne Haug
Alma Center, Wisconsin

Dinner-In-A-Dish

1 1-lb. 7-oz. can syrup-packed sweet
   potatoes
1 No. 2 can sliced apples
1 can luncheon meat, sliced
¼ c. packed brown sugar
½ tsp. each cinnamon, thyme

Cut sweet potatoes in half lengthwise. Alternate layers of potatoes and apples in 2-quart baking dish. Arrange luncheon meat on top. Sprinkle with remaining ingredients. Bake at 400 degrees for 25 minutes. Yield: 4 servings.

Sister M. Aloysius
Sious Falls, South Dakota

Sunday Supper Casserole

8 slices bread
2 tbsp. butter
1 12-oz. can luncheon meat, shredded
1 sm. onion, shredded
½ lb. American cheese, sliced
3 eggs, beaten
½ tsp. salt
Few drops of Tabasco sauce
2½ c. milk

Spread bread with butter. Cut each slice into 6 strips. Mix luncheon meat and onion in bowl. Alternate layers of bread, meat mixture and cheese in greased baking dish. Beat eggs with seasonings and milk. Pour over layers. Bake at 350 degrees for 1 hour. Serve at once. Yield: 4 servings.

Martha Lee Atlas
Batesville, Mississippi

Tasty One-Dish Meal

1 pkg. frozen mixed vegetables
1 can luncheon meat, sliced
1 c. cream of mushroom soup
⅓ c. milk
¼ tsp. Worcestershire sauce
½ c. dry bread crumbs
2 tbsp. butter, melted
Paprika

Separate vegetables. Place in 1½-quart casserole. Top with meat slices. Dilute soup with milk in small saucepan. Add Worcestershire sauce. Heat to boiling, stirring constantly. Pour over meat and vegetables. Toss crumbs with butter; sprinkle over sauce. Sprinkle with paprika. Bake at 375 degrees for 30 minutes. Yield: 4-5 servings.

Dorothy M. Ham
Nahunta, Georgia

Audra's Sausage Casserole

1½ lb. mild pork sausage
4 or 5 green onions, chopped
1 lg. green pepper, chopped
1 stalk celery and leaves, chopped
2 pkg. chicken noodle soup mix
1 c. cooked rice
1 sm. can water chestnuts, sliced

Saute sausage in skillet, stirring to crumble; drain. Saute next 3 ingredients in pan drippings until tender. Add remaining ingredients with 4½ cups water. Simmer for 15 minutes. Turn into casserole. Bake, covered, at 350 degrees for 1½ hours. Yield: 6 servings.

Audra Carolyn Smallwood
Irvine, Kentucky

Baked Sausage Lasagna

1 lb. Italian sausage
1 clove of garlic, minced
3 tbsp. parsley flakes
1 tbsp. basil
3½ tsp. salt
1 1-lb. can tomatoes
2 6-oz. cans tomato paste
3 c. cream-style cottage cheese
2 eggs, beaten
½ tsp. pepper
½ c. grated Parmesan cheese
10 oz. lasagna noodles, cooked
1 lb. mozzarella cheese, sliced

Brown sausage slowly in skillet. Spoon off excess drippings. Add garlic, 1 tablespoon parsley, basil, 1½ teaspoons salt, tomatoes and tomato paste. Simmer for 30 minutes, stirring occasionally. Combine cottage cheese with eggs, remaining seasonings and Parmesan cheese in bowl. Alternate layers of noodles, cottage cheese mixture, mozzarella cheese and sauce in 9 × 13-inch baking dish until all ingredients are used. Bake at 375 degrees for 30 minutes. Garnish with triangles of mozzarella cheese. Let stand for 10 to 15 minutes before serving.

Laura Van De Mark
McLouth, Kansas

Baked Sausage and Corn

1 lb. sausage links
1 No. 303 can cream-style corn
½ tsp. dry mustard
¼ c. milk
2 eggs, beaten
¼ c. chopped green pepper
1 sm. onion, chopped

Parboil sausage in water in saucepan for 10 minutes; drain. Mix corn, mustard, milk, eggs, pepper and onion in bowl. Place mixture in greased 1½-quart casserole. Arrange sausage links on corn mixture. Bake at 350 degrees for 1 hour. Yield: 4 servings.

Mrs. Edward Swift
Middleboro, Massachusetts

Corn-Sausage Pie

1 lb. link sausage
3 tbsp. chopped green pepper
2 tbsp. chopped onion
3 tbsp. flour
1 tsp. salt
¾ c. milk
2 beaten eggs
1 No. 2 can cream-style corn
1 recipe biscuit dough

Brown sausage in skillet; set aside. Saute green pepper and onion in 4 tablespoons sausage drippings. Blend in flour and salt; remove from heat. Blend in milk, eggs and corn. Cook until mixture is heated through, stirring constantly. Pour into casserole. Arrange sausage in spoke pattern in center of casserole. Spoon biscuit dough around edge. Bake at 425 degrees for 20 minutes. Yield: 4-6 servings.

Thelma House
Claremont, New Hampshire

Jambalaya Jamboree

½ lb. fresh mushrooms, sliced
¼ c. butter
1 1-lb. can French-style green beans, drained
½ c. minute rice
1 1-lb. can stewed tomatoes
¼ tsp. salt
½ lb. brown-and-serve sausage
½ c. shredded sharp Cheddar cheese

Saute mushrooms in butter in skillet until tender. Add green beans; sprinkle rice over beans. Cover with tomatoes; season with salt. Cover. Simmer for 20 minutes or until rice is tender. Cook sausage in skillet until brown; drain. Place sausage on tomatoes; sprinkle cheese over sausage. Heat for 5 minutes or until cheese is melted. Yield: 6 servings.

Susan Carothers
Murrysville, Pennsylvania

Mexican Luncheon Dish

1 lb. sausage
1 c. diced onions
Diced jalapeno peppers to taste
1 c. diced green pepper
1 8-oz. package elbow macaroni
1 1-lb. can tomatoes
1 c. sour cream
1 c. milk
2 tbsp. sugar
1 tbsp. chili powder
1 tsp. salt

Saute sausage in skillet until brown; drain off excess drippings. Add onions, jalapeno peppers and green pepper. Saute until onion is transparent. Add macaroni, tomatoes, sour cream, milk, sugar, chili powder and salt. Cover. Simmer for 20 to 25 minutes or until macaroni is tender. Yield: About 8 servings.

Donna Samuelson
Monahans, Texas

Pineapple-Sausage Ring with Tangy Sauce

1 lb. smoked sausage links, fried
5 pineapple rings
1 jar pimento
2 c. flour
1 tsp. salt
2 tsp. baking powder
½ tsp. sage
¼ c. shortening
2 eggs
¾ c. milk
Tangy Sauce

Layer ⅔ of the sausage, all pineapple and several pimento pieces in casserole. Combine flour, salt, baking powder, and sage in bowl. Cut in shortening until crumbly. Slice remaining sausage and pimento into flour mixture.

Beat eggs and milk together in bowl. Stir into dry ingredients. Spoon around edge of casserole. Bake at 400 degrees for 30 to 45 minutes or until brown. Serve with Tangy Sauce.

Tangy Sauce

1½ tbsp. melted butter
3 tbsp. flour
⅓ tsp. salt
¼ tsp. paprika
1½ c. milk
¼ lb. grated Velveeta cheese

Combine first 4 ingredients in saucepan. Add milk gradually. Cook over low heat until slightly thickened, stirring constantly. Add cheese. Cook until cheese melts. Yield: 6 servings.

Lilla Schmeltekopf
Burleson, Texas

Risotto

2½ c. consomme
1 c. rice
½ c. chopped green pepper
½ c. chopped onion
½ c. drained sliced mushrooms
½ c. sliced pepperoni
1 tbsp. oil
3½ c. canned tomatoes
1 tsp. salt
6 oz. mozzarella cheese, shredded

Bring consomme to a boil in saucepan. Add rice; cover. Cook over low heat for 25 minutes or until liquid is absorbed. Saute green pepper, onion, mushrooms and pepperoni in oil in skillet. Add tomatoes and salt. Layer rice and vegetables in casserole. Top with cheese. Bake at 350 degrees for 20 minutes.

Elizabeth Nichols
Salem, Oregon

Santa's Midnight Casserole

1 lb. link sausage
2½ c. medium white sauce
Worcestershire sauce to taste
½ lb. Cheddar cheese, cubed
1 can button mushrooms, drained
8 hard-boiled eggs

Brown sausages in skillet; drain on paper towel. Cut sausages in half. Heat white sauce; season with Worcestershire sauce. Fold in sausages, cheese and mushrooms. Pour into 1½-quart casserole. Press eggs into sausage mixture. Refrigerate overnight. Bake in 375-degree oven for 45 minutes to 1 hour. Yield: 8 servings.

Sheila Hall
Montgomery, Alabama

Saturday Night Special

2 c. rice
3 pkg. chicken-noodle soup mix
3 c. diced celery
1 lg. onion, chopped
1 lg. green pepper, chopped
2 lb. sausage, cooked, drained
1 can boned chicken
½ c. blanched almonds

Combine rice, soup mix and 9 cups water in large saucepan. Bring to a boil. Cover; reduce heat. Cook until rice is tender. Saute celery, onion, green pepper and sausage in skillet for 5 minutes. Add sausage mixture to rice. Stir in chicken and almonds. Pour into large casserole. Bake at 350 degrees for 1 hour. Yield: 25-30 servings.

Carol Scrimshaw
Calgary, Alberta, Canada

Sausage and Rice Bake

1 lb. sausage
1 c. each chopped onions, celery
1 green pepper, chopped
1 clove of garlic, minced
1 c. rice
1 can cream of mushroom soup
2 cans cream of chicken soup
½ c. grated cheese

Brown sausage; pour off drippings. Add onions, celery, green pepper and garlic. Simmer until tender. Add remaining ingredients except cheese. Pour into baking dish. Sprinkle cheese on top. Bake at 350 degrees for 1½ hours. Yield: 6 servings.

Mrs. C. D. Huston
Greenwood, Mississippi

Vegetables

Artichoke Hearts and Pecans

2 No. 2 cans artichoke hearts, drained
1 c. half and half
2 tbsp. butter
2 tbsp. flour
Salt and pepper to taste
Tabasco sauce to taste
½ c. broken pecans
¼ c. bread crumbs
2 tbsp. grated Parmesan cheese

Place artichoke hearts in casserole.. Combine half and half, butter and flour in saucepan. Cook until thickened, stirring constantly. Season with salt, pepper and Tabasco sauce. Pour sauce over artichoke hearts; add pecans. Sprinkle with bread crumbs and cheese. Bake at 300 degrees until bubbly. Yield: 6 servings.

Selma Sailors
Diller, Nebraska

Breaded Asparagus Casserole

1 10-oz. package frozen asparagus cuts
½ c. canned sliced mushrooms, drained
2½ tbsp. butter
2½ tbsp. flour
1 c. milk
¼ tsp. salt
Pepper to taste
¼ tsp. grated onion
2 hard-boiled eggs, chopped

Cook asparagus using package directions; drain. Saute ¼ cup mushrooms in butter in skillet until light brown. Remove skillet from heat. Add flour; blend well. Stir in milk gradually. Cook over medium heat until thickened, stirring comstantly. Add salt, pepper and onion; mix well. Layer asparagus, egg and reserved mushrooms in 1-quart casserole. Top with sauce. Bake at 300 degrees for 10 minutes or until bubbly. Yield: 4 servings.

Sharon Hill
Corning, Iowa

Baked Green Beans and Mushrooms

2½ c. bread cubes
½ c. melted butter
4 3-oz. cans sliced mushrooms, drained
3 15½-oz. cans cut green beans, drained
¼ tsp. salt
⅛ tsp. pepper
⅔ tbsp. chopped onion
2 cans cream of mushroom soup
1 c. milk
½ c. toasted sliced almonds

Combine bread cubes with butter. Place half the mixture in greased 13 × 9 × 2-inch casserole. Add mushrooms and beans; sprinkle with salt, pepper and onion. Combine soup and milk in bowl, blending well. Pour over vegetables. Top with almonds. Bake at 350 degrees until bubbly.

Eloise Taylor
Hastings, Nebraska

Italian Green Bean Bake

1 15-oz. can tomato sauce
2 1-lb. can green beans, drained
1 tbsp. instant minced onion
2 tsp. sugar
¼ tsp. Worcestershire sauce
¼ tsp. oregano
4 oz. mozzarella cheese, shredded

Combine all ingredients except half the mozzarella cheese. Place in baking dish. Top with remaining cheese. Bake at 350 degrees for 30 minutes. Yield: 6-8 servings.

Deborah J. Crook
McGuffey, Ohio

Swiss Green Beans

4 tsp. grated onion
½ lb. mushrooms, sliced
½ sm. green pepper, finely chopped
4 tbsp. butter
2 tbsp. flour
½ tsp. salt
¼ tsp. pepper
3 tsp. sugar
1 c. sour cream
2 cans whole green beans, drained
2 c. grated Swiss cheese
Buttered crumbs

Saute onion, mushrooms and green peppers in 2 tablespoons butter in skillet until tender. Blend in next 5 ingredients. Heat through but do not boil, stirring constantly. Stir in green beans and cheese. Place in greased casserole. Top with buttered crumbs; dot with remaining butter. Bake at 350 degrees for 20 minutes.

Bette D. Jenness
Linesville, Pennsylvania

Cranberry Baked Beans

1½ c. dried lima beans
1½ tsp. salt
2 c. cranberry juice cocktail
⅓ c. chopped onion
2 tbsp. molasses
1 tsp. dry mustard
⅛ tsp. ginger
¼ c. catsup
2 tbsp. dark brown sugar
¼ lb. salt pork, sliced

Combine beans with remaining ingredients except salt pork in bowl; mix well. Layer bean mixture with salt pork in 2-quart casserole. Add 1½ cups reserved bean liquid. Bake, covered, at 250 degrees for 5 to 7 hours. Uncover. Bake 1 hour longer, adding more reserved liquid if necessary to prevent dryness. Yield: 6-8 servings.

Hallie Watson
Batavia, New York

Broccoli A La Teggart

2 pkg. frozen broccoli spears
¼ c. butter
¼ c. flour
1 c. milk
½ c. chicken consomme
½ c. white wine
Salt and pepper to taste
1 can French-fried onion rings
½ c. slivered almonds
½ c. grated sharp cheese

Cook broccoli using package directions; drain. Place in 1½-quart casserole. Melt butter in saucepan; blend in flour. Add milk and consomme. Cook until thickened, stirring constantly. Remove from heat; stir in wine, salt and pepper. Pour over broccoli. Top with onion rings; sprinkle with almonds and cheese. Bake at 375 degrees for 30 minutes. Yield: 8-10 servings.

Beatrice Carmichael
Washington, Pennsylvania

Broccoli-Corn Casserole

2 pkg. frozen broccoli, thawed
2 cans cream-style corn

1 egg, beaten
1 c. bread crumbs
1 c. grated Cheddar cheese

Combine broccoli, corn and egg in bowl; mix well. Place in casserole. Top with bread crumbs. Bake at 350 degrees for 45 minutes. Sprinkle cheese on top. Bake 15 minutes longer or until cheese is melted.

Diane Intoccio
Reynoldsburg, Ohio

Party Broccoli and Onions

2 pkg. frozen broccoli spears, thawed
1 pkg. frozen chopped broccoli, thawed
3 cans cream of mushroom soup
½ c. grated Cheddar cheese
2 c. whole pearl onions
½ c. slivered almonds
Bread crumbs
Butter

Place broccoli in casserole. Combine soup, cheese, onions and almonds in bowl; mix well. Spread over broccoli. Top with bread crumbs; dot with butter. Bake in 350-degree oven for 35 minutes or until bubbly. Yield: 20 servings.

Jamie H. White
Signal Mountain, Tennessee

Nutty Brussels Sprouts Au Gratin

2 10-oz. packages frozen Brussels sprouts
½ c. grated process sharp cheese
¼ c. butter
¼ c. herb-seasoned stuffing mix
⅓ c. chopped walnuts

Cook Brussel sprouts using package directions; drain. Place in greased 1½-quart casserole. Sprinkle with cheese. Melt butter in skillet; add stuffing mix. Saute until lightly browned, stirring constantly. Spoon over casserole. Bake at 400 degrees for 10 minutes or until cheese is melted. Yield: 6 servings.

Bernadette Schoen
East Troy, Wisconsin

Belmont Casserole

3 c. shredded cabbage, cooked
1½ c. drained canned tomatoes
Salt and paprika to taste
1 c. grated cheese
1 c. bread crumbs
1½ tbsp. butter

Alternate layers of cabbage and tomatoes in greased casserole, sprinkling each layer with salt and paprika. Top with cheese and bread crumbs; dot with butter. Bake at 250 degrees for 15 minutes or until cheese melts. Yield: 6 servings.

Fornadia Cook
Marietta, Georgia

Scalloped Cabbage Casserole

4 c. chopped cabbage
1½ c. grated American cheese
1½ c. cracker crumbs
Salt and pepper to taste

Place cabbage in saucepan with 1½ tablespoons water; cover. Cook over low heat until just wilted. Layer half the cabbage in buttered 9 × 13-inch baking dish with half the cheese and cracker crumbs. Season with salt and pepper. Repeat layers. Bake in 350-degree oven for 30 minutes.

Nancy Stearley
Bloomfield, Indiana

Guess Again Casserole

2 lb. carrots, peeled, sliced
2 tbsp. margarine
1 med. onion, grated
6 to 8 oz. Cheddar cheese, grated
Salt and pepper to taste
Buttered bread crumbs (opt.)

Cook carrots in a small amount of water in saucepan until tender; drain. Mash carrots in bowl. Add remaining ingredients except bread crumbs; mix well. Pour into casserole. Top with bread crumbs. Bake at 350 degrees for 40 minutes. Yield: 8 servings.

Marjorie Little
Pembroke, Massachusetts

Peachy Carrots

2 c. sliced carrots
1 can peach pie filling
½ tsp. salt
½ tsp. cinnamon
1 tbsp. butter

Cook carrots in a small amount of boiling salted water in saucepan until tender-crisp; drain. Combine with pie filling, salt and cinnamon in bowl; mix well. Pour into greased casserole. Dot with butter. Bake, covered, at 350 degrees for 25 minutes.

Helen Hollinger
Celina, Ohio

Scalloped Carrot Casserole

1 med. onion, chopped
Margarine
4 c. sliced cooked carrots
1 can cream of celery soup
½ tsp. salt
Dash of pepper
½ c. grated Cheddar cheese
3 c. herb-seasoned stuffing mix

Brown onion in 3 tablespoons margarine in skillet. Add carrots, soup, salt, pepper and cheese; mix well. Melt ½ cup margarine; toss with stuffing mix. Layer carrot mixture and stuffing mixture in casserole, ending with stuffing mixture. Bake at 350-degrees for 45 minutes.

Lois J. Smeltzer
Mysterstown, Pennsylvania

Company Cauliflower

2 tsp. sesame seed, toasted
1 med. head cauliflower
Salt and pepper to taste
1 c. sour cream at room temperature
1 c. shredded Cheddar cheese

Rinse cauliflower; separate into flowerets. Cook in 1-inch salted water in covered saucepan until tender; drain. Season with salt and pepper. Layer half the cauliflower, sour cream, cheese and sesame seed in casserole. Repeat layers. Bake at 350 degrees for 20 minutes or until heated through.

Rebecca B. Johnson
Chattanooga, Tennessee

Far-East Celery Casserole

4 c. 1-inch celery pieces
1 5-oz. can water chestnuts, sliced, drained
¼ c. diced pimento
1 c. cream of chicken soup
1 c. bread crumbs
¼ c. toasted almonds
4 tbsp. melted butter

Cook celery in a small amount of boiling salted water in saucepan until tender-crisp; drain. Combine with water chestnuts, pimento and soup in bowl; mix well. Spoon into lightly greased casserole. Top with bread crumbs and almonds. Drizzle with butter. Yield: 6 servings.

Charlene Woodruff
Winston, North Dakota

Baked Corn with Sour Cream

6 strips crisp-cooked bacon, crumbled
2 tbsp. chopped onion
2 tbsp. butter
2 tbsp. flour
½ tsp. salt
1 c. sour cream
2 12-oz. cans whole kernel corn
1 tbsp. chopped parsley

Saute onion in butter in large skillet. Blend in flour and salt. Add sour cream gradually, stirring until smooth. Bring to a boil; add corn. Cook until heated through. Fold in half the bacon. Pour into greased baking dish. Top with parsley and remaining bacon. Bake at 350 degrees for 30 minutes or until bubbly. Yield: 6-8 servings.

Effie Gish
Ft. Worth, Texas

Corn and Onion Casserole

1 3½-oz. can French-fried onions
½ c. chopped green pepper
1 tsp. butter
1 1-lb. can cream-style corn
2 tsp. chopped pimento
1 egg, slightly beaten

Crush half the onions. Saute green pepper in butter in skillet until tender. Add corn, pimento, egg and crushed onions; mix well.

Pour into 1½-quart casserole. Bake at 350 degrees for 25 minutes or until firm. Sprinkle with remaining onions. Bake for 5 minutes longer.

Brownie S. Babington
Franklinton, Louisiana

Old-Fashioned Corn Pudding

2 tbsp. honey
1 c. milk
1½ tbsp. flour
3 eggs, beaten
1 1-lb. can cream-style corn
2 tbsp. melted butter
½ tsp. salt
Dash of allspice

Blend honey and milk together in bowl; add flour gradually, stirring until smooth. Add eggs, corn, butter and salt; mix well. Turn into greased 1-quart baking dish. Sprinkle with allspice. Place baking dish in pan of hot water. Bake at 300 degrees for 1¾ hours or until custard is set. Yield: 6 servings.

Mary F. Dunn
Byers, Texas

Favorite Baked Cucumbers

¼ c. chopped onion
¼ c. chopped parsley
½ c. margarine
1½ c. bread crumbs
2 c. tomato pulp
1 tsp. salt
⅛ tsp. pepper
4 lg. cucumbers, peeled and sliced

Saute onion and parsley in margarine until onion is transparent. Add remaining ingredients except cucumbers. Cook for 5 minutes longer. Reserve part of onion mixture for topping. Arrange cucumber slices and remaining onion mixture in layers in greased casserole. Pour in a small amount of hot water. Spread reserved onion mixture over top. Bake at 350 degrees for 1 hour or until cucumbers are tender and top is browned. Yield: 4-6 servings.

Dorothy W. Hayes
Roanoke, Virginia

Eggplant California

1 med. yellow onion, coarsely chopped
3 tbsp. butter
1 lg. eggplant, peeled
½ c. beef broth
2 med. firm tomatoes, peeled
1 tsp. seasoned salt
1 tsp. pepper
1 c. sour cream
½ tsp. oregano
2 tsp. chopped chives
⅔ c. soft bread crumbs

Saute onion in 2 tablespoons butter in skillet until tender, not brown. Cut eggplant into 1-inch cubes. Add to onion; cook for several minutes, stirring frequently. Stir in broth. Spoon half the eggplant into buttered 2-quart casserole. Layer half the tomatoes, seasonings and sour cream over eggplant. Repeat layers. Melt remaining butter; toss with crumbs. Sprinkle over casserole. Bake at 350 degrees for 20 to 25 minutes or until brown. Yield: 6 servings.

Agnes Warner
Olean, New York

Eggplant Casserole with Cheese Sauce

1 eggplant, peeled, diced
Salt
Butter
4 tbsp. flour
½ tsp. cayenne pepper
1 c. milk
½ lb. sharp cheese, grated
Bread crumbs

Boil eggplant in salted water in saucepan until tender-crisp; drain well. Blend butter, flour, ¼ teaspoon salt, cayenne pepper and milk in saucepan. Cook until thick, stirring constantly. Remove from heat; stir in cheese until melted. Place eggplant in casserole; cover with cheese sauce. Top with bread crumbs; dot with additional butter. Bake at 350 degrees until heated through. Yield: 6-8 servings.

Maurine Taylor
Gilmer, Texas

Green Pepper Casserole

4 to 5 green peppers, chopped
1 tbsp. butter, melted
2 tbsp. flour
1 c. milk
¾ c. grated cheese
½ c. cracker crumbs

Cook green pepper in a small amount of boiling salted water in saucepan until tender; drain. Blend butter and flour in saucepan; stir in milk gradually. Cook until thick, stirring constantly. Add cheese; stir until melted. Add peppers. Pour into baking dish; top with crumbs. Bake at 350 degrees until brown. Yield: 5-6 servings.

Martha Young
Franklin, Kentucky

Mushroom Garden Bake

1 lb. fresh mushrooms, halved
1 lb. cherry tomatoes
¼ lb. zucchini, sliced
1 tsp. Italian seasoning
1 tsp. onion powder
¼ tsp. garlic powder
1 tsp. salt
⅛ tsp. pepper
3 tbsp. olive oil
2 tbsp. melted butter

Line 8 × 10-inch baking dish with foil. Layer vegetables evenly in foil. Combine seasonings in small bowl; mix well. Sprinkle over vegetables. Combine oil and butter in small bowl; mix well. Sprinkle over vegetables. Cover with foil, sealing tightly. Bake at 350 degrees for 25 to 30 minutes. Toss vegetables lightly before serving. Yield: 6 servings.

Jewell T. Johnson
Albany, Georgia

Baked Onion Rings

2 lb. white onions, sliced
8 slices buttered toast
¼ lb. American cheese, shredded
2 eggs, beaten
2 c. milk
½ tsp. salt
⅛ tsp. pepper
1 tbsp. butter
Paprika (opt.)

Cook onions in boiling salted water until tender; drain well. Place half the toast in baking dish. Layer half the onions and half the cheese over toast. Repeat layers. Beat eggs with milk, salt and pepper. Pour over cheese. Dot with butter; sprinkle with paprika. Bake at 350 degrees for 40 minutes or until set. Yield: 8 servings.

Mrs. Ron Havenstein
Iowa City, Iowa

Onions Au Gratin

2 lb. small onions, peeled
1 c. sharp grated cheese
1 can cream of mushroom soup
1 tbsp. Worcestershire sauce
Dash of Tabasco sauce
Croutons

Cook onions in boiling salted water until tender. Drain in colander for about 30 minutes. Arrange onions in buttered baking dish; sprinkle with cheese. Mix soup and sauces; pour over cheese. Top with croutons. Bake in 350-degree oven until brown and bubbly.

Norma Francis Bachschmid
Hurst, Texas

Parsnips in Orange Sauce

12 sm. parsnips, cooked
½ c. orange juice
2 tbsp. brown sugar
2 tbsp. light syrup
½ tsp. salt
⅛ tsp. paprika
2 tbsp. butter
Grated orange peel

Place parsnips in shallow 9 × 12-inch casserole. Combine orange juice, brown sugar, syrup, salt and paprika. Pour over parsnips. Dot with butter; sprinkle with orange peel. Bake at 400 degrees for 20 minutes or until bubbly. Yield: 6 servings.

Bette Eckre Johnson
Raymond, Minnesota

Green Peas Au Gratin

2 pkg. frozen peas
2 5-oz. cans water chestnuts, drained, sliced
1 can cream of mushroom soup
1½ c. grated sharp Cheddar cheese

Cook peas using package directions; drain well. Combine peas, water chestnuts and soup;

mix gently. Stir in cheese. Place in lightly greased casserole. Bake at 350 degrees for 25 to 30 minutes or until bubbly. Yield: 6-8 servings.

Joyce Niedenthal
Fort Lauderdale, Florida

Sunday Company Casserole

1 pkg. frozen green peas
1 can water chestnuts, drained, sliced
2 4-oz. cans mushroom stems and pieces
1 can bean sprouts, drained
1 can cream of mushroom soup
½ lb. Cheddar cheese, grated
1 can French-fried onion rings

Cook peas using package directions; drain. Drain mushrooms; reserve liquid. Place peas, bean sprouts, mushrooms and water chestnuts in 9-inch casserole. Mix reserved mushroom liquid with soup in saucepan; heat through. Add to pea mixture; mix well. Sprinkle with cheese. Bake, covered, in 350-degree oven for 30 minutes. Place onion rings on top. Bake for 15 minutes longer.

Mrs. Irvin Lepien
Clayton, Wisconsin

Confetti Potato Puff

1 3-oz. envelope instant mashed potatoes
¼ c. chopped pimento
¼ c. chopped green onions
1 clove of garlic, minced
2 tsp. salt
2 c. cottage cheese
1 c. sour cream
3 egg yolks, well beaten
3 egg whites, stiffly beaten
2 tbsp. butter

Prepare potatoes using package directions, add pimento, onions, garlic, salt, cottage cheese, sour cream and egg yolks. Fold in egg whites. Place in greased 2-quart casserole. Dot with butter. Bake at 350 degrees for 1 hour. Yield: 8 servings.

Frances Bowyer
Fayetteville, North Carolina

Creamy Cheese Potatoes

1¼ c. milk
1 8-oz. package cream cheese, softened
1 tbsp. snipped chives
½ tsp. instant minced onion
¼ tsp. salt
4 c. cubed cooked potatoes
Paprika

Blend milk into cream cheese in medium saucepan over low hat. Stir in chives, onion and salt. Add potatoes; stir carefully to coat. Turn into 1½-quart casserole; sprinkle with paprika. Bake in 350-degree oven for 30 minutes. Yield: 5-6 servings.

Jane A. Bower
Crescent City, California

Hashed Brown Casserole

1 2-lb. bag frozen hashed brown
    potatoes
1 can cream of chicken soup
2 tbsp., each chopped onion, pimento,
    bell pepper
1 8-oz. carton sour cream
1 stick butter, melted

Combine all ingredients in bowl. Place in greased casserole. Bake in 325-degree oven for 2 hours.

Betsy Mowery
Longview, Texas

Mushroom-Scalloped Potatoes

1 can cream of mushroom soup
¾ c. grated American cheese
¼ c. finely chopped pimento
½ tsp. salt
⅔ c. evaporated milk
4 c. thinly sliced potatoes

Combine soup, ½ cup cheese, pimento and salt in bowl. Stir in milk and potatoes gradually. Place in greased baking dish. Top with remaining cheese. Bake at 350 degrees for 1 hour. Yield: 6 servings.

Kathleen Koskella
Mt. Home, Idaho

Potato-Onion Casserole

3 med. potatoes
1 tsp. seasoned salt

½ c. sour cream
½ c. Cheez Whiz
½ can French-fried onion rings

Cook potatoes in boiling water to cover until tender. Drain; mash. Add next 3 ingredients and beat until fluffy. Place in greased casserole. Bake at 350 degrees for 20 minutes. Top with onion rings. Bake for 4 minutes longer or until onions are toasted.

Sarah McCreight
Morganton, North Carolina

Potato Souffle

4 servings instant mashed potatoes
1 tbsp. finely chopped onion
1 tsp. monosodium glutamate
½ tsp. salt
6 eggs, separated

Prepare potatoes using package directions. Add next 3 ingredients and beaten egg yolks; mix well. Beat egg whites until stiff peaks form. Fold into egg yolk mixture. Turn into 2-quart casserole. Bake at 375 degrees for 35 minutes. Yield: 6 servings.

Carol White
Longview, Texas

Baked Spinach with Sour Cream

3 10-oz. packages frozen chopped
    spinach
1 pkg. dry onion soup mix
1 pt. sour cream

Cook spinach using package directions; drain well. Combine onion soup mix and sour cream; mix well. Stir sour cream mixture into spinach. Place in baking dish. Bake, covered, at 350 degrees for 30 minutes or until bubbly. Yield: 8 servings.

Mable Wallmark
Mead, Washington

Spinach-Cheese Bake

1 10-oz. package frozen, chopped
    spinach
1 c. cooked rice
1½ c. shredded sharp American cheese
2 eggs, slightly beaten
2 tbsp. soft butter
⅓ c. milk
2½ tbsp. chopped onion

½ tsp. Worcestershire sauce
1 tsp. salt
¼ tsp. crushed rosemary

Cook spinach using package directions; drain. Add remaining ingredients; mix well. Pour into 6 × 10-inch baking dish. Bake at 350 degrees for 20 to 25 minutes or until knife inserted in center comes out clean. Yield: 6 servings.

Karen Orsak
Hull, Massachusetts

Spinach Souffle

1 c. chopped spinach
2 tbsp. chopped onion
¼ c. cottage cheese
1 egg white, stiffly beaten

Cook spinach and onion in saucepan over low heat until spinach is tender, stirring frequently; drain well. Stir in cottage cheese. Fold in egg white. Pour into small ungreased baking pan. Bake in 350-degree oven for 20 to 25 minutes or until set.

Virginia T. Bond
Madison, West Virginia

Squash Casserole Deluxe

5 c. sliced yellow squash
½ c. chopped onion
2 tsp. salt
1 c. grated carrots
1 carton sour cream
1 can cream of celery soup
½ c. melted margarine
1 pkg. herb-seasoned stuffing mix

Cook squash and onion in water with salt for 5 minutes. Drain; set aside. Combine next 3 ingredients with ¼ cup margarine and half the stuffing mix in bowl; mix well. Layer squash and carrot mixtures alternately in 9 × 12-inch baking dish. Spread remaining stuffing mix on top. Drizzle with remaining margarine. Bake at 350 degrees for 20 minutes. Yield: 6-8 servings.

Sandra Vincent
Forsyth, Missouri

Squash Piquant

1 pkg. frozen squash
1 tbsp. butter
1 slice bacon

½ tsp. salt
¼ tsp. each pepper, sugar
¼ c. chopped onion
1 tbsp. chopped green pepper (opt.)
¾ c. crushed cracker crumbs
1 egg, beaten

Cook squash using package directions. Drain; mash with butter. Fry bacon in skillet until crisp. Drain and crumble, reserving pan drippings. Add all ingredients to drippings, mixing well. Pour into baking dish. Bake at 350 degrees for 30 to 40 minutes.

Flora Fry
Coleman, Texas

Yellow Squash Casserole

4 c. sliced yellow squash
1 med. onion, sliced
2 med. carrots, grated
1 c. sour cream
½ c. milk
1 8-oz. package herb-seasoned stuffing mix
Salt and pepper to taste
½ c. melted butter

Cook squash and onion in boiling water until tender. Drain; mash. Add carrots, sour cream, milk and half the stuffing mix; mix well. Season with salt and pepper. Mix remaining stuffing mix with butter. Alternate layers of squash mixture and buttered stuffing in baking dish ending with stuffing. Bake at 350 degrees for 30 to 40 minutes or until brown.

Elizabeth Green
Loretto, Tennessee

Scalloped Sweet Potatoes and Apples

2 c. sliced boiled sweet potatoes
1½ c. thinly sliced sour apples
½ c. packed brown sugar
¼ c. butter
1 tsp. salt

Layer half the first 3 ingredients in buttered casserole. Dot with half the butter; add half the salt. Repeat with remaining ingredients. Bake at 350 degrees for 1 hour.

Mary Irish
Shawano, Wisconsin

Special Sweet Potato Casserole

3 c. mashed sweet potatoes
¾ c. sugar
½ tsp. salt
2 eggs, beaten
½ c. milk
½ tsp. vanilla extract
Margarine
1 c. packed brown sugar
⅓ c. flour
1 c. coconut

Combine first 6 ingredients with ½ cup melted margarine in bowl; mix well. Pour into casserole. Mix remaining ingredients with 3 tablespoons margarine in bowl. Spread over sweet potato mixture. Bake at 350 degrees for 35 minutes.

Emily Rickman
Richmond, Virginia

Cheesy Macaroni-Tomato Pie

1½ c. flour
1 tsp. salt
Butter
⅔ c. creamed cottage cheese
2 c. elbow macaroni, cooked, drained
2 c. milk
2 tbsp. chopped parsley
⅛ tsp. pepper
1 3-oz. package cream cheese, softened
2½ c. shredded Cheddar cheese
1 lg. tomato, sliced

Combine 1¼ cups flour and salt in medium bowl. Cut in ½ cup butter until crumbly. Stir in cottage cheese. Form dough into ball. Wrap in waxed paper. Refrigerate for 30 minutes. Roll out between waxed paper to ⅛-inch thickness. Remove top paper. Invert into 1-inch pie plate. Remove remaining paper. Trim to ½ inch from edge. Fold under; flute. Spread bottom with 1 teaspoon softened butter. Melt ¼ cup butter in saucepan; blend in ¼ cup flour. Stir in milk gradually. Cook until thick, stirring constantly. Add parsley, pepper and cream cheese, stirring until cheese is melted. Reserve ¾ cup Cheddar cheese. Alternate layers of macaroni, Cheddar cheese and cheese sauce in cottage cheese crust until all ingredients are used. Top with reserved Cheddar cheese. Bake at 400 degrees for 30 minutes or until crust is brown. Cut tomato slices into halves; arrange over pie.

Bake for 5 minutes longer. Let stand for 10 minutes before serving. Yield: 8 servings.

Picture for this recipe on page 4.

Green Tomato Casserole

4 green tomatoes, sliced
1 tsp. salt
½ tsp. pepper
2 tsp. butter
1 c. grated cheese
1 c. cracker crumbs

Place layer of tomatoes in lightly greased casserole. Sprinkle with salt and pepper; dot with butter. Add ⅓ of the cheese. Repeat layers 2 times. Bake in 350-degree oven for 30 to 40 minutes. Sprinkle cracker crumbs over top. Dot with additional butter. Bake for 5 minutes longer. Yield: 4 servings.

Sarah A. McCreight
Morganton, North Carolina

Tomato-Cheese Bake

4 med. tomatoes, peeled, quartered
1 tsp. sugar
Dash of pepper
2 c. shredded sharp process American
    cheese
½ c. finely chopped celery
¼ c. finely chopped onion
1 c. soft bread crumbs
2 tbsp. margarine, melted

Sprinkle tomatoes with sugar and pepper. Toss cheese, celery and onion in bowl. Place half the tomato in 6 × 10 inch baking dish. Sprinkle half the cheese mixture over tomato. Repeat layers. Toss bread crumbs with margarine. Sprinkle over casserole. Bake at 350 degrees for 25 to 30 minutes. Yield: 4-6 servings.

Paula Pope
Columbus, Ohio

Creamy Turnip Casserole

6 med. turnips, peeled, quartered
¼ tsp. caraway seed
Salt
½ c. sour cream
Dash of cayenne pepper
¼ tsp. sweet basil
1 tsp. grated lemon rind
⅓ c. buttered bread crumbs

Cook turnips with caraway seed in boiling salted water to cover until tender. Drain well. Place in buttered casserole. Heat sour cream with dash of salt. Pour over turnips. Sprinkle with remaining ingredients. Bake at 400 degrees for 10 to 12 minutes.

Sister Alphonsa Masterson
Nevada, Missouri

Turnip Souffle

2 lb. turnips, cubed
1 onion, chopped
3 tbsp. butter
1 can cream of mushroom soup
¾ tsp. salt
½ tsp. pepper
3 eggs well-beaten
Bread crumbs
Parmesan cheese

Cook turnips and onion in small amount of water in saucepan until tender. Drain and mash. Add remaining ingredients except crumbs and cheese. Pour into buttered casserole. Sprinkle with bread crumbs and Parmesan cheese. Bake in 350-degree oven for 30 minutes.

Agnes Foster
Frankfort, Kentucky

Cheesy Zucchini Bake

2 c. bread crumbs
1 clove of garlic, crushed
1 tsp. sweet basil
1 tsp. rosemary
1 tsp. parsley
½ tsp. salt
¼ tsp. pepper
5 sm. zucchini, thinly sliced
1 c. grated Parmesan cheese
½ c. oil

Combine first 7 ingredients in bowl, mixing well. Place half the zucchini in greased 9 × 9-inch baking dish. Cover with half the crumb mixture and half the cheese. Sprinkle with 4 tablespoons oil. Repeat layers. Bake at 375 degrees for 1 to 1½ hours or until golden brown. Yield: 6 servings.

Deborah Block
Plymouth, Massachusetts

Tomato-Zucchini Scallop

6 or 7 zucchini, sliced
4 or 6 med. tomatoes, sliced
1 lg. onion, sliced
Salt and pepper to taste
1 to 2 c. croutons
1 c. grated cheese

Layer zucchini, onion, tomatoes, salt and pepper in greased 1½-quart casserole. Sprinkle with croutons. Repeat layers. Top with tomato slices. Bake, covered, at 350 degrees for 1 hour. Uncover; sprinkle with cheese. Return to oven to melt cheese.

Clarabel Tepe
Fort Towson, Oklahoma

Zucchini in Cream

6 sm. zucchini, cut into ½-in. slices
⅔ c. sour cream
1 tbsp. butter
½ tsp. seasoned salt
6 tbsp. grated sharp Cheddar cheese
3 tbsp. fresh bread crumbs

Simmer zucchini in water to cover for 10 minutes; drain. Spread in 8-inch baking dish. Combine sour cream, butter, seasoned salt and 4 tablespoons cheese in small saucepan. Heat slowly, stirring until blended. Pour over zucchini. Top with bread crumbs and remaining cheese. Bake at 375 degrees for 10 minutes or until golden. Let stand for 5 minutes before serving.

Ardis East
El Paso, Texas

Layered Vegetable Casserole

3 med. yellow squash, sliced
1 lb. mushrooms, sliced
1 tbsp. butter
10 oz. spinach, cooked
2 lg. slices mozzarella cheese
¼ c. grated Parmesan cheese

Cook squash in a small amount of boiling salted water until first tender; drain. Saute mushrooms in butter in skillet; set aside. Layer squash, 1 slice mozzarella cheese, mushrooms, 1 slice mozzarella and spinach in casserole. Sprinkle with Parmesan cheese. Bake at 400 degrees for 20 to 25 minutes until bubbly.

Mary Scullion Carter
Cleveland, Tennessee

1 c. finely rolled cracker crumbs
3 tbsp. melted butter
1 tsp. marjoram
½ tsp. onion powder

Place soup mix in medium bowl; stir in 1 cup boiling water. Blend in sour cream and cheese. Add vegetables. Pour into 1½-quart baking dish. Combine next 4 ingredients; sprinkle over vegetable mixture. Bake in 350-degree oven for 30 to 35 minutes or until bubbly. Yield: 6 servings.

Loretta Spurlock
Chattanooga, Tennessee

Mary's Favorite Casserole

2 tbsp. butter, melted
1 tsp. onion powder
1⅓ c. crushed Corn Chex
2 cans cream of mushroom soup
½ c. milk
¼ tsp. salt
¼ tsp. onion juice
Dash of Tabasco sauce
1 2-oz. can mushrooms
1 10-oz. package frozen peas, thawed, drained
2 lb. tiny new potatoes, cooked, peeled

Combine butter and onion powder in skillet over low heat. Stir in cereal until coated; set aside. Combine soup with next 4 ingredients in bowl; blend well. Stir in mushrooms, peas and potatoes. Pour into 2-quart buttered baking dish. Top with crumbs. Bake at 325 degrees for 45 minutes. Yield: 4 servings.

Picture for this recipe above.

Savory Vegetable Casserole

2 env. instant cream of mushroom soup mix
½ c. sour cream
½ c. grated Swiss cheese
2 1-lb. cans mixed vegetables, drained

Trio Casserole

1 10-oz. package frozen green peas
1 10-oz. package frozen French-style green beans
1 10-oz. package frozen baby lima beans
1 tbsp. Worcestershire sauce
1 tsp. prepared mustard
Juice of ½ lemon
1 sm. purple onion, grated
1 can water chestnuts, sliced, drained
1½ c. mayonnaise
Bread crumbs, buttered

Cook vegetables separately using package directions; drain. Combine all vegetables with next 6 ingredients in buttered casserole. Sprinkle with bread crumbs. Bake at 350 degrees for 30 minutes. Yield: 10 servings.

Elizabeth Miller
Shelby, North Carolina

Yam-Corn Combo

4 med. Louisiana yams, cooked, mashed
1 17-oz. can cream-style corn
2 oz. Swiss cheese, cubed
Dash of pepper
2 eggs, beaten
¾ c. sliced pimento-stuffed olives
1 3-oz. can French-fried onions

Combine first 5 ingredients with ½ cup olives and half the French-fried onions in bowl; blend well. Pour into 1½-quart casserole; sprinkle with remaining onions. Bake at 350 degrees for 40 minutes. Top with remaining olives. Bake for 5 minutes longer. Garnish with parsley. Yield: 6 servings.

Picture for this recipe on page 75.

Fast and Simple

Batter-Up Beef Casserole

¼ c. butter
1½ c. self-rising flour
1½ c. milk
1 c. grated Cheddar cheese
2 tbsp. finely chopped onion
1 tbsp. sugar
2½ c. beef stew

Melt butter in 8-inch square baking pan. Combine all ingredients except stew in bowl. Stir until blended. Pour batter into pan. Pour beef stew over batter. Do not stir. Bake in 350-degree oven for about 1 hour or until golden brown. Yield: 6 servings.

Miriam Toth
Castro Valley, California

Easy Chinese Pepper Steak

1 lb. beef round steak, cubed
¼ c. shortening
Dash of garlic powder
3 tbsp. soy sauce
1 tbsp. brown sugar
1 16-oz. can mixed Chinese vegetables, drained
1 16-oz. can tomatoes and juice
2 green peppers, coarsely chopped
1 sm. onion, chopped
2 tbsp. cornstarch

Stir-fry steak in shortening in skillet. Add garlic powder, soy sauce and brown sugar; mix well. Cook, covered, over high heat for 5 minutes. Add next 4 ingredients; mix well. Cook for 5 minutes longer. Blend cornstarch with ¼ cup cold water. Stir into cooked mixture. Cook until thickened stirring constantly.

Judy Adler
Snyder, Oklahoma

Grandmother's Hash-in-a-Hurry

1 12-oz. can corned beef, ground
2 med. onions, ground
8 med. potatoes, ground
¼ c. shortening
1 tsp. salt
Pepper to taste

Combine corned beef, onions and potatoes in bowl; mix well. Melt shortening in skillet. Add corned beef mixture. Season with salt and pepper. Add 1 cup water. Cook, covered, for 45 minutes or until onions and potatoes are tender, stirring frequently. Remove cover; cook until lightly browned. Yield: 16 servings.

Carolyn Fillmore Fredrick
Brighton, Michigan

Japanese Beef and Vegetables

Oil
¼ c. Sherry
¼ c. soy sauce
1 clove of garlic, crushed
½ tsp. minced fresh ginger
1½ lb. beef round, slivered
2 c. diagonally sliced celery
2 c. diagonally sliced carrots
½ lb. mushrooms, sliced
1 c. beef stock
¼ c. sliced water chestnuts
2 tbsp. cornstarch

Combine ¼ cup oil with next 4 ingredients in bowl. Add beef; stir to coat. Marinate in refrigerator for 1 to 2 hours; drain, reserving marinade. Brown beef in 3 tablespoons oil in skillet. Remove; set aside. Stir-fry celery and carrots until celery is bright green. Remove; set aside. Saute mushrooms until golden. Add marinade, beef, vegetables and stock; mix well. Simmer, covered, for 15 minutes. Stir in water chestnuts. Blend cornstarch with a small amount of cold water until smooth. Stir into mixture. Cook until thickened, stirring constantly.

Sherri Day
Anchorage, Alaska

Simple Spinach-Beef Casserole

1 c. sliced mushrooms
2 tbsp. butter
1 10-oz. package frozen chopped spinach, cooked, drained
1 8-oz. package narrow noodles, cooked
2 tbsp. melted butter
Salt and pepper to taste
1½ c. diced cooked beef
1½ c. sour cream
1 c. buttered bread crumbs

Saute mushrooms in butter in skillet until tender. Add spinach; mix well. Combine noodles, melted butter, salt and pepper in bowl. Mix beef and sour cream together in bowl. Arrange half the noodles in greased

2-quart casserole. Spread sour cream mixture on top. Cover with spinach mixture. Top with remaining noodles. Sprinkle with crumbs. Bake at 350 degrees for 30 minutes. Yield: 6 servings.

Doris Malo
Mountain View, California

Chili Twist

2 c. egg noodles, cooked
2 15½-oz. cans chili con carne
1 tbsp. parsley flakes
½ tsp. sweet basil
¼ tsp. oregano
2 8-oz. cans tomato sauce

Combine all ingredients in large saucepan; mix well. Cook until heated through. Yield: 4-6 servings.

Darlene La Borde
Richland, Washington

Mexi-Chili Casserole

1 6-oz. package corn chips
2 c. shredded sharp, processed American cheese
1 15-oz. can chili with beans
1 15-oz. can enchilada sauce
1 8-oz. can seasoned tomato sauce
1 tbsp. instant minced onion
1 c. sour cream

Reserve 1 cup corn chips and ½ cup cheese. Combine remaining chips and cheese with all ingredients except sour cream in bowl; mix well. Pour into casserole. Bake at 375 degrees for 20 minutes. Top with sour cream. Sprinkle with reserved cheese. Arrange remaining corn chips around edge. Bake for 5 minutes longer. Yield: 6 servings.

Betty Herbel
Belcourt, North Dakota

Speedy Beef Goulash

1 lb. lean ground beef
1 med. onion, chopped
1 med. green pepper, chopped
1 tsp. salt
¼ tsp. pepper
1 8-oz. can tomato sauce
1 can whole kernel corn

Saute ground beef, onion and green pepper in skillet until brown. Stir in salt, pepper and tomato sauce. Simmer, covered for 15 to 20 minutes. Add corn. Heat through. Yield: 6 servings.

Mary Ray White
Troup, Texas

Busy Day Casserole

¾ lb. ground beef
1 c. macaroni
1 29-oz. can whole tomatoes
½ c. catsup
⅓ c. finely chopped onion
⅓ c. finely chopped green pepper
1 tsp. salt
¼ tsp. pepper

Brown ground beef in skillet, stirring until crumbly. Add remaining ingredients. Cover. Cook for 25 minutes or until macaroni is tender. Yield: 6 servings.

Brenda Brandt
Paw Paw, Michigan

Ground Beef and Sour Cream Skillet

1 lb. ground beef
1 c. chopped onion
3 c. tomato juice
1½ tsp. celery salt
2 tsp. Worcestershire sauce
Dash of pepper
½ 5-oz. package noodles
¼ c. chopped green pepper
1 c. sour cream
1 3-oz. can mushrooms

Saute ground beef with onion in large skillet until crumbly. Combine next 4 ingredients in bowl; mix well. Layer noodles over ground beef; add tomato juice mixture. Cover. Simmer over low heat for 20 minutes. Add green pepper. Cook for 10 minutes longer. Add sour cream and mushrooms; mix well. Serve immediately.

Mary S. Hatcher
Quitman, Georgia

Hasty Hamburger Heaven

1 lb. ground beef
1 c. fine noodles
1 No. 2 can tomatoes
1 c. finely chopped onions
1 c. diced green peppers
1 c. chopped celery
1 4-oz. can mushroom stems and pieces
1 c. ripe olives, sliced
¼ tsp. garlic salt
¼ lb. Cheddar cheese, shredded

Brown ground beef in skillet, stirring until crumbly. Layer remaining ingredients except cheese in order given over ground beef. Cook, covered, over low heat for 25 minutes. Sprinkle with cheese. Yield: 6 servings.

Margaret McIntosh
Lostant, Illinois

Easy Macaroni and Beef Casserole

1 lb. ground beef
1 med. onion, chopped
1 stalk celery, chopped
2 tsp. salt
Dash of monosodium glutamate
¼ tsp. pepper
1 20-oz. can tomatoes
1½ c. macaroni, cooked
½ c. bread crumbs (opt.)

Brown ground beef in skillet, stirring until crumbly. Pour off excess drippings. Add onion and celery. Cook for 5 minutes longer. Add remaining ingredients except bread crumbs; mix well. Simmer until heated through. Top with crumbs.

Mrs. S. McDonald
British Columbia, Canada

Macaroni Skillet Supper

1 lb. lean ground beef
¾ c. chopped onion
½ c. chopped celery
¼ c. chopped green pepper
2 tbsp. butter
1 28-oz. can tomatoes
1 tsp. salt
¼ tsp. pepper
1 c. elbow macaroni
½ c. grated Parmesan cheese

¾ c. shredded Cheddar cheese
Chopped parsley

Saute ground beef, onion, celery and green peppers in butter in skillet until browned. Add tomatoes, salt and pepper. Bring to a boil; add macaroni. Cook, covered, over low heat for 10 minutes or until macaroni is tender, stirring occasionally. Stir in Parmesan cheese; sprinkle with Cheddar cheese. Let stand, covered, for 5 minutes. Sprinkle with parsley. Yield: 6 servings.

Picture for this recipe on page 91.

Poor Man's Hot Dish

1 lb. ground beef
1 sm. onion, chopped
Salt and pepper to taste
1 can tomato soup
1 head cabbage, cut into chunks

Saute ground beef and onion in skillet until brown. Season with salt and pepper; blend in soup. Add cabbage; mix lightly. Cook over low heat for 30 minutes or until cabbage is tender. Yield: 4-6 servings.

Judith Evans
Wamsutter, Wyoming

Quickie Skillet Spaghetti

1 lb. ground beef
1 sm. onion, chopped
1 c. spaghetti, broken into 1-in. pieces
1 clove of garlic, chopped (opt.)
1 c. catsup
¼ tsp. pepper
1 tsp. salt
¼ tsp. thyme
2½ c. tomato juice

Brown ground beef with onion in skillet, stirring until crumbly. Add remaining ingredients; mix well. Simmer, covered, for 45 minutes. Yield: 6 servings.

Nadia Hamilton
Harbor Creek, Pennsylvania

Quick Tamale Pie

½ lb. ground beef
½ c. chopped onion
2 tbsp. shortening
1 can whole kernel corn
1 can tomatoes

Sailor's Supper

2 lb. ground beef
2 tsp. salt
½ tsp. pepper
1 lg. onion, sliced thin
1 No. 2½ can tomatoes
1 No. 303 can whole kernel corn
1 15-oz. can tomato sauce
1 tbsp. chili powder
2 c. fine noodles

Season ground beef with salt and pepper. Saute with onion in skillet until brown. Add remaining ingredients; mix well. Simmer, covered, for 20 minutes. Remove cover. Cook for 10 minutes longer. Yield: 8 servings.

Diane Yakos
Versailles, Ohio

Stove Top Hamburger Casserole

1 lb. green beans
1 lb. extra lean ground beef
1 med. onion, chopped
8 to 10 lg. fresh mushrooms, sliced
2 beef bouillon cubes
Chopped tomatoes (opt.)
Parmesan cheese to taste

Cook green beans until tender; drain, reserving liquid. Saute beef in skillet until brown. Add onion and mushrooms. Cook until onion is tender. Stir in green beans. Dissolve bouillon cubes in reserved bean liquid; stir into beef mixture. Add tomatoes; sprinkle with Parmesan cheese. Cover. Steam for several minutes to blend flavors.

Joan McCown
Columbus, Ohio

½ tbsp. chili powder
1 tsp. salt
½ c. cornmeal
½ c. flour
1 tbsp. sugar
1 tsp. baking powder
1 c. milk
1 egg

Brown ground beef and onion in shortening in skillet, stirring until crumbly. Add next 3 ingredients with ½ teaspoon salt. Cook for 15 minutes. Pour into baking dish. Combine remaining ingredients with ½ teaspoon salt in bowl; mix well. Pour over ground beef mixture. Bake at 425 degrees for 25 to 30 minutes.

Mildred Bridi
Surveyor, West Virginia

Scramble

1 lb. ground beef
1 sm. onion, chopped
3 tbsp. olive oil
1 sm. can sliced mushrooms
1 pkg. frozen spinach
Salt and pepper to taste
6 eggs, well beaten

Saute ground beef with onions in olive oil in skillet until crumbly. Stir in mushrooms and spinach. Season with salt and pepper. Pour eggs over ground beef mixture. Cook until eggs set, stirring gently. Yield: 6 servings.

Mitzi Funk
Crescent City, California

Thirty-Minute Noodle Dinner

1 lb. ground beef
1 onion, chopped
1 6-oz. package medium noodles
1 10-oz. can mushroom soup

Saute beef and onion in skillet until browned. Arrange noodles over beef mixture. Combine soup with 1 soup can water; pour over noodles. Do not stir. Simmer until noodles are tender, stirring occasionally. Add more water if necessary. Yield: 4-5 servings.

Carolyn Rose
Amherst, Ohio

Witch's Brew

1 lb. ground beef
1 lg. onion, sliced (opt.)
1 can pork and beans
1 can sliced mushrooms
1 c. catsup
Salt and pepper to taste

Brown hamburger and onion in skillet, stirring until crumbly. Stir in remaining ingredients. Heat through. Yield: 4 servings.

Lena Bell Moore
Vegreville, Alberta, Canada

Easy Deviled Ham Casserole

1   4½-oz. can deviled ham
¾ tsp. paprika
2 tsp. flour
1¾ c. light cream
1 tbsp. grated onion
¾ tsp. salt
¼ tsp. pepper
2 No. 2 cans green beans, drained
1 No. 2 can whole kernel corn, drained
½ c. sour cream

Saute deviled ham in skillet until heated, stirring constantly. Add next 6 ingredients. Cook until thickened, stirring constantly. Add vegetables and sour cream; mix well. Simmer until heated through. Yield: 6 servings.

Hilda Harman
Smithville, Mississippi

Quick Egg Noodles with Pork Sauce

1½ lb. boneless pork shoulder
1 tbsp. flour
1 tbsp. oil
½ c. chopped celery
½ c. chopped green pepper
1 clove of garlic, minced
1 tsp. salt
½ tsp. monosodium glutamate
⅛ tsp. pepper
1 onion bouillon cube
1 1-lb. can green beans
½ c. sour cream
8 oz. medium egg noodles, cooked
½ tsp. caraway seed (opt.)
Paprika
Chopped parsley

Cut pork into 2 × ½-inch strips; toss with flour. Brown in hot oil in large skillet; drain. Add celery, green pepper and garlic. Cook for 3 minutes. Stir in salt, monosodium glutamate, pepper and bouillon cube. Drain beans, reserving liquid. Add enough water to reserved liquid to measure 1 cup. Add to pork mixture. Cover. Simmer for 40 to 45 minutes or until pork is tender. Stir in beans and sour cream. Heat through. Stir in noodles. Sprinkle with remaining ingredients. Yield: 4-6 servings.

Midge Cornwallis
Lexington, Kentucky

Tasty Ham A La King

4 tbsp. diced onion
1 6-oz. can mushrooms
2 tbsp. diced celery (opt.)
2 tbsp. diced green pepper (opt.)
4 tbsp. margarine
2 c. white sauce
2 to 2½ c. diced cooked ham
2 tsp. pimento
3 c. cooked rice

Saute first 4 ingredients in margarine in skillet until tender. Blend in white sauce. Stir in ham and pimento. Cook over low heat for 12 to 15 minutes. Stir in rice.

Ruth Yelvington
Corsicana, Texas

Old-Fashioned But Easy Gumbo

2 or 3 sm. slices salt pork
1 c. corn
1 c. green limas
2 c. sliced fresh okra
6 tomatoes, quartered
Sugar to taste
Salt and pepper to taste

Fry salt pork in skillet until crisp; add corn and lima beans with ¾ cup water. Cook for 10 minutes stirring occasionally. Add remaining ingredients. Simmer, covered, for 30 minutes, stirring occasionally. Yield: 4 servings.

Dorothy W. Reese
Atlanta, Georgia

Chili-in-a-Hurry

6 to 8 slices bacon, diced
1 c. rice
4 c. canned tomatoes
¼ lb. Cheddar cheese, grated
1 tbsp. sugar
1 tbsp. chili
½ tsp. salt

Saute bacon in skillet until tender but not crisp. Stir in remaining ingredients with ½ cup hot water. Simmer, covered, until rice is tender.

Helen Purvis
Cranbrook, British Columbia, Canada

Chicken and Almonds

1 c. sliced bamboo shoots
1 c. chopped celery
1 c. chopped onions
8 water chestnuts, sliced
6 tbsp. oil
½ lb. blanched almonds
1 lb. chicken, boned, cubed
¾ tsp. salt
2 tbsp. cornstarch
3 tbsp. soy sauce
2 tbsp. Sherry
1 tsp. sugar
¼ c. chicken stock
Cooked rice

Saute first 4 ingredients in 3 tablespoons oil in skillet. Remove. Brown almonds; drain. Coat chicken with mixture of salt, cornstarch, soy sauce, Sherry and sugar. Add remaining oil to skillet. Saute chicken until tender. Add stock. Heat through. Add vegetables and almonds. Serve on rice. Yield: 6 servings.

Melba Smith
Grandview, Texas

Chicken-Chili-Cheese Casserole

12 corn tortillas
1 can cream of mushroom soup
1 can chicken soup
1 c. milk
1 can green chili sauce
4 lg. chicken breasts, cooked, boned
1 lb. Cheddar cheese, grated
1 onion, chopped
Melted butter

Cut each tortilla into 8 wedges. Combine soups, milk and chili sauce. Layer tortillas, chicken, cheese, onion and soup mixture into greased baking dish until all ingredients are used, ending with tortillas. Drizzle butter over top. Refrigerate for 24 hours. Bake at 300 degrees for 1½ hours. Yield: 8 servings.

Susan Farling
Paducah, Kentucky

Double-Time Chow Mein

1 onion, chopped
1 stick margarine, melted
2 sm. cans chicken
2 cans cream of mushroom soup
2 cans cream of chicken soup
1 sm. jar sliced pimento
1 lg. can chow mein noodles

Saute onion in margarine in Dutch oven. Add remaining ingredients in order given, reserving half the noodles. Top with reserved noodles. Bake at 350 degrees for 20 minutes or until brown and bubbly.

Cecile Poling
Houston, Texas

Margaret's Easy Chicken Casserole

4 c. diced cooked chicken
4 c. diced celery
1 c. toasted slivered almonds
1 tsp. salt
4 tbsp. grated onion
4 tbsp. lemon juice
2 c. mayonnaise
1 c. grated American cheese
2 c. crushed potato chips

Mix chicken, celery, almonds, salt, onion, lemon juice and mayonnaise together in bowl. Turn into casserole. Top with grated cheese and potato chips. Bake at 350 degrees for 10 minutes or until cheese is melted. Yield: 8 servings.

Margaret Tisdale
Memphis, Tennessee

Peanutty Chicken Casserole

2 c. chopped cooked chicken
½ c. chopped celery
2 hard-boiled eggs, sliced
1 tbsp. minced onion
1 c. cream of mushroom soup
¼ c. mayonnaise
2 tbsp. lemon juice
¼ c. chopped peanuts
Crushed potato chips

Mix all ingredients except potato chips together in bowl. Place in casserole. Top with potato chips. Bake at 350 degrees for 30 minutes. Yield: 4-6 servings.

Mrs. Gershon Kuster
Fort Defiance, Virginia

Perfect Chicken Casserole

1 can chicken soup
½ c. milk
1 can boned chicken
2 c. cooked noodles
2 tbsp. diced pimento
1 tbsp. chopped parsley
2 tbsp. buttered bread crumbs

Blend soup and milk in 1½-quart casserole. Add chicken, noodles, pimento and parsley. Sprinkle crumbs on top. Bake at 375 degrees for 25 minutes. Yield: 4 servings.

Mrs. Francis Reeves
Hutchins, Texas

Simple Salad Casserole

6 oz. chicken
1 can cream of mushroom soup
1 c. diced celery
2 tsp. minced onion
½ c. almonds
½ tsp. salt
¼ tsp. pepper
¾ c. salad dressing
3 hard-boiled eggs, chopped
2 c. crushed potato chips

Combine all ingredients except potato chips in bowl; mix well. Pour into casserole. Top with potato chips. Bake at 425 degrees for 15 to 20 minutes. Yield: 4-6 servings.

Marilyn C. Anderson
Hoffman, Minnesota

Quick Chicken Tetrazzini

1 sm. onion, chopped
2 tbsp. each chopped green pepper, celery
1 tbsp. margarine
1 8-oz. can boned chicken
1 can cream of mushroom soup
1 box chicken and noodles dinner, cooked

Saute onion, green pepper and celery in margarine in skillet. Add chicken, soup and chicken and noodles dinner. Turn into casserole. Bake at 325 degrees for 25 minutes. Yield: 6 servings.

Helen L. Scott
Haynesville, Louisiana

Last-Minute Company Chicken

¼ c. melted margarine
1 c. cracker crumbs
2 c. diced cooked chicken
1 c. sour cream
1 can cream of chicken soup
¼ c. broth
Salt and pepper to taste

Combine margarine and cracker crumbs in bowl; blend well. Spoon half the crumbs into shallow 2-quart casserole. Cover with chicken. Combine sour cream, soup, broth, salt and pepper in bowl; blend well. Pour over chicken. Top with remaining crumbs. Bake in 350-degree oven for 20 to 25 minutes. Yield: 6 servings.

Mrs. Phil Addy
Plains, Georgia

Souper Chicken Crunch

2 c. chopped cooked chicken
1 c. chopped celery
½ c. slivered almonds
2 hard-boiled eggs, sliced
2 tbsp. Worcestershire sauce
¼ c. mayonnaise
1 can cream of chicken soup
1 c. crushed potato chips

Combine all ingredients except potato chips in bowl; mix well. Place in 1½ quart casserole. Top with potato chips. Bake at 350 degrees for 30 minutes. Yield: 8 servings.

Virginia C. Taylor
Springville, Alabama

Tomato-Broccoli Chicken

2 lg. chicken breasts, boned
Salt and pepper
¼ c. chopped onion
2 tbsp. margarine
1 10-oz. package frozen cut broccoli,
  thawed
1 tsp. lemon juice
¼ tsp. thyme, crushed
3 med. tomatoes, cut in wedges

Cut chicken into ½-inch strips. Cook with onion in margarine in medium skillet until chicken is no longer pink. Stir in remaining ingredients except tomatoes. Simmer, covered, for 6 minutes. Add tomatoes. Simmer, covered, for 3 to 4 minutes longer. Yield: 4 servings.

Jolene Hartman
Lancaster, Texas

Turkey-Ham Royale

1 med. onion, minced
4 tbsp. margarine
¼ c. flour
2 tsp. dry mustard
1 tsp. salt
¼ tsp. curry powder
2 tbsp. catsup
½ tsp. Worcestershire sauce
2½ c. milk
1⅔ c. evaporated milk
2 c. diced cooked turkey
2 c. diced cooked ham

Saute onion in margarine in large saucepan until golden. Remove from heat. Blend in next 6 ingredients; add milk and evaporated milk gradually. Cook over low heat until thick, stirring constantly. Boil for 1 minute; stir in turkey and ham. Yield: 8 servings.

Irene Robotham
Bellaire, Michigan

Can Opener Casserole

1 1-lb. can green beans, drained
1 1-lb. can salmon, drained
1½ c. shredded Cheddar cheese
¼ c. flour
2 tbsp. instant minced onion
1 can tomato soup
½ c. milk
1 tsp. parsley flakes
1 recipe baking powder biscuit dough

Place beans, salmon and 1 cup cheese in 2½-quart casserole. Sprinkle with flour and 1 tablespoon onion. Add soup and milk; stir gently. Add remaining cheese, onion and parsley flakes to biscuit dough. Drop by spoonfuls around edge of casserole. Bake in 450-degree oven for 25 to 30 minutes.

Karen Tinseth
Sauk Rapids, Minnesota

Cantonese Shrimp and Beans

1½ tsp. chicken bouillon
¼ c. thinly sliced green onion
1 clove of garlic, crushed
1½ lb. frozen uncooked shrimp, thawed
1 tbsp. oil
Salt to taste
1 tsp. ginger
Dash of pepper
1 9-oz. package frozen cut green beans
1 tbsp. cornstarch

Dissolve bouillon in 1 cup boiling water. Saute onion, garlic and shrimp in oil in skillet for 3 minutes adding a small amount of bouillon to prevent sticking if necessary. Stir in next 4 ingredients with bouillon. Simmer, covered, for 5 minutes or until beans are tender-crisp. Blend cornstarch with 1 tablespoon cold water. Add to shrimp mixture. Cook until thick and clear, stirring constantly.

Lynne Belmont
Dallas, Texas

Chinese-Fried Rice

Dash of pepper
2 eggs, slightly beaten
1 to 2 tbsp. chopped green onion
4 c. cooked rice
2 tbsp. soy sauce
½ tsp. sugar
1 c. chopped cooked shrimp

Stir pepper into eggs. Pour into hot non-stick skillet. Cook until eggs begin to set. Add remaining ingredients; stir to blend well. Cook until heated through, stirring gently.

Elaine Skurdal
Fisher, Minnesota

Five-Can Casserole

1 can cream of chicken soup
1 6½-oz. can tuna
1 can cream of mushroom soup
1 can chow mein noodles
1 5-oz. can evaporated milk
Bread crumbs

Combine all ingredients except bread crumbs in 1-quart casserole. Sprinkle bread crumbs on top. Bake for 1 hour at 350 degrees. Yield: 4 servings.

Janet White Stafford
Hanover, Illinois

Garden Harvest Shrimp Casserole

1 med. eggplant, peeled
1½ tbsp. lemon juice
4 med. cloves of garlic, minced
½ c. olive oil
2 lg. sweet onions, thinly sliced
1 tbsp. salt
½ tsp. freshly ground pepper
5 med. green peppers, cut in strips
5 sm. zucchini, thinly sliced
2 lb. large shrimp
2 lg. tomatoes, thinly sliced

Slice eggplant ¼ inch thick; sprinkle with lemon juice. Cut shrimp in half lengthwise. Saute garlic in ¼ cup olive oil in large skillet for 1 minute. Add onions. Cook for 1 minute longer, season lightly with salt and pepper. Remove from skillet. Alternate layers of onion mixture, green peppers, eggplant, zucchini, shrimp and tomatoes, sprinkling each layer with olive oil. Simmer, covered, for 20 minutes. Uncover. Cook for 10 minutes longer or until vegetables are tender. Yield: 6 servings.

Mary Cummings
Johnson City, Tennessee

Jiffy Shrimp Curry

1 tbsp. butter
1 can cream of shrimp soup, thawed
1 c. sour cream
2 tbsp. instant minced onion
½ tsp. curry powder
1 can tuna, drained, flaked
Hot cooked rice

Combine butter and soup in skillet. Heat until blended, stirring constantly. Add remaining ingredients blending well. Heat, covered, until bubbly. Stir in rice. Yield: 4-6 servings.

Anita H. Lewis
Oley, Pennsylvania

Shrimp Amandine

1 c. blanched slivered almonds
½ c. butter, melted
1 1-lb. package frozen shrimp, thawed
Dash of pepper
2 tbsp. chopped parsley

Saute almonds in butter until lightly browned; remove. Add shrimp; saute until lightly browned. Add seasonings, parsley and almonds. Garnish with toast points. Yield: 6 servings.

Ouida M. Shows
Theodore, Alabama

Shrimp Creole Orleans

¾ c. chopped onions
1 clove of garlic, minced
1 c. chopped green pepper
3 c. sliced celery
¼ c. butter
1 29-oz. can tomatoes
3 tbsp. brown sugar
1½ tsp. salt
⅛ tsp. pepper
1 tsp. thyme
2 bay leaves, crumbled
2 lb. fresh cleaned shrimp
2 tbsp. lemon juice
3 c. hot cooked rice

Saute onions, garlic, green pepper and celery in butter in skillet until tender. Add next 6 ingredients; mix well. Simmer for 15 minutes. Stir in shrimp and lemon juice. Simmer for 6 to 8 minutes longer. Stir in rice. Yield: 6 servings.

Caroline Bode
San Antonio, Texas

Asparagus-Water Chestnut Casserole

1 can sliced water chestnuts
1 8-oz. can sliced mushrooms
1 sm. jar chopped pimentos
4 hard-boiled eggs, chopped
1 can cream of mushroom soup
2 cans asparagus spears, drained
1 can French-fried onion rings

Drain first 3 ingredients. Mix with eggs and soup. Layer asparagus in greased casserole. Bake at 350 degrees for 20 minutes. Top with onion rings. Bake for 10 minutes longer. Yield: 6-8 servings.

Mary Ada Parks
Anna, Illinois

California Rice

1 c. canned tomatoes
5 slices bacon, diced
½ c. diced celery
4 oz. mushrooms, sliced
¾ c. grated Cheddar cheese
1 env. onion soup mix
1⅓ c. instant rice

Drain tomatoes, reserving juice. Add enough water to juice to measure 1⅓ cups. Fry bacon until crisp; drain, reserving 2 tablespoons bacon drippings. Saute celery and mushrooms in drippings until tender. Stir in ½ cup cheese, tomato juice and remaining ingredients. Pour into 1½-quart baking dish. Top with remaining cheese. Bake, covered, at 375 degrees for 20 minutes. Yield: 4 servings.

Lila Zobac
Cornell, Wisconsin

Club Mushroom Casserole

1 lb. fresh mushrooms, sliced
½ c. butter
⅓ c. flour
3 c. milk
2 tsp. Worcestershire sauce
1½ tsp. salt
¼ tsp. pepper
4 hard-boiled eggs, sliced
½ c. diced green pepper
1 4-oz. can pimento, diced
2 c. shredded process cheese

Saute mushrooms in butter. Blend in flour; add milk gradually. Cook until thickened, stirring constantly. Fold in remaining ingredients except cheese. Pour into greased casserole. Bake at 350 degrees for 30 minutes or until brown. Top with cheese. Yield: 6-8 servings.

Jean Capling
Warren, Michigan

Easy Egg and Vegetable Casserole

2 c. canned mixed vegetables, drained
6 hard-boiled eggs, coarsely chopped
⅓ c. finely chopped onion
½ c. sliced olives
¼ c. chopped pimento
1 can cream of mushroom soup
½ tsp. salt
¼ c. crushed Shredded Wheat
¼ c. shredded Cheddar cheese

Combine first 7 ingredients in 1-quart casserole; mix well. Sprinkle with remaining ingredients. Bake at 350 degrees until bubbly. Yield: 6 servings.

Paula Calhoun
Fisher, Illinois

Fireside Macaroni Casserole

1 8-oz. package macaroni, cooked
½ c. mayonnaise
¼ c. diced green pepper
¼ c. chopped pimento
1 sm. onion, chopped
½ tsp. salt
1 can mushroom soup
½ c. cream
1 c. grated sharp cheese

Combine all ingredients in large bowl; mix well. Pour into casserole. Bake at 325 degrees for 30 minutes or until bubbly.

Venita Gill
Ft. Worth, Texas

Fast Four-Way Casserole

1 6-oz. package wide noodles, cooked
1 carton cottage cheese
1 carton sour cream
¼ c. milk
1 c. cubed Cheddar cheese
1 tbsp. chopped pimento
¼ tsp. Worcestershire sauce
¼ tsp. salt

Combine all ingredients in large bowl; toss to mix. Place in buttered casserole. Bake at 325 degrees for 20 to 30 minutes. Garnish with olives.

Patricia Johnson
Gadsden, Alabama

Garden Skillet-in-a-Hurry

2 sm. zucchini, sliced
½ c. chopped onion
½ tsp. basil leaves, crushed
2 tbsp. butter
1 11-oz. can condensed Cheddar cheese
    soup
3 c. cooked elbow macaroni
2 c. shredded sharp Cheddar cheese
1 16-oz. can tomatoes, chopped,
    well-drained
½ tsp. prepared mustard

Saute zucchini and onion with basil in butter in skillet until tender. Add remaining ingredients. Heat until cheese melts, stirring occasionally. Yield: 4-6 servings.

Elisa Grover
Seattle, Washington

Mock Noodles Romanoff

1 6-oz. package noodles, cooked
1 c. cottage cheese
1 c. sour cream
1 tsp. minced onion
1 sm. clove of garlic, minced
½ tsp. salt
1 tsp. Worcestershire sauce
¼ c. grated cheese

Combine first 7 ingredients in bowl; mix well. Spoon into greased 2-quart casserole; sprinkle with cheese. Bake at 350 degrees for 40 minutes.

Myrtle Stevens
Ninnekah, Oklahoma

Quick Quiche

1½ c. grated Swiss cheese
8 slices crisp-cooked bacon, crumbled
1 9-in. pastry shell, chilled
3 eggs, slightly beaten
1 c. heavy cream
½ c. milk
½ tsp. each salt, dry mustard
¼ tsp. pepper

Sprinkle cheese and bacon in pastry shell. Blend remaining ingredients in bowl. Pour over cheese mixture. Bake at 375 degrees for 45 minutes or until knife inserted in center comes out clean. Cut into wedges; serve hot. Yield: 6 servings.

Ethel M. Poley
Narrowsburg, New York

Simple Broccoli Casserole

1 pkg. frozen, chopped broccoli, thawed
1 pkg. frozen, chopped spinach, thawed
1 c. shredded Cheddar cheese
1 pt. large-curd cottage cheese
3 eggs, beaten
3 tbsp. flour
Salt to taste
Dry bread crumbs
Butter

Drain vegetables well. Combine with next 5 ingredients in bowl; mix well. Place in buttered baking dish. Sprinkle with bread crumbs; dot with butter. Bake at 350 degrees for 1 hour. Yield: 6 servings.

Debbie Hopkins
Arp, Texas

Waffley Cheese Strata

1 9-oz. package frozen waffles
2 tbsp. butter, softened
½ lb. Cheddar cheese, thinly sliced
Paprika
6 eggs, beaten
3 c. milk
½ tsp. salt
¼ tsp. cayenne pepper
6 tomato slices

Prepare waffles using package directions; cool on wire rack. Butter waffles. Alternate layers of waffles and cheese in buttered 8 × 12-inch baking dish ending with cheese. Sprinkle with paprika. Beat eggs with milk, salt and cayenne pepper in large bowl. Pour evenly over waffles and cheese. Refrigerate for 3 to 4 hours. Bake at 325 degrees for 35 minutes. Top with tomato slices. Bake for 10 to 15 minutes longer. Yield: 6 servings.

Picture for this recipe on page 87.

Microwave and Crock•Pot

Chinese Potted Veal

1 lb. chopped veal
1 egg
¼ c. seasoned bread crumbs
1 tsp. soy sauce
½ tsp. garlic powder
2 c. tomato juice

Combine first 5 ingredients in bowl; mix well. Shape into small balls. Place in glass casserole; add tomato juice. Cover. Microwave on High for 20 minutes, stirring twice. Yield: 4-6 servings.

Adelaide Larsen
Provo, Utah

Full of Boloney

1½ c. diced potatoes
1½ c. cubed bologna
2 tbsp. minced green pepper
1 can cream of celery soup
2 lg. slices cheese, quartered

Combine all ingredients except cheese in 1½-quart glass casserole. Cover. Microwave on High for 15 minutes. Top with cheese. Microwave for 30 seconds longer or until cheese melts. Yield: 4 servings.

Esther Wonderlich
Mount Pleasant, Iowa

Microwave Quiche

4 eggs
1 c. cream
2 c. seasoned stuffing mix
½ lb. ground chuck
1 tsp. Worcestershire sauce
1 tsp. salt
2 c. sliced green onions, including tops
1 c. shredded Swiss cheese
3 or 4 drops of hot pepper sauce
Paprika to taste

Beat 1 egg slightly in large mixing bowl. Add ½ cup cream and stuffing mix. Toss lightly. Let stand until most of liquid is absorbed. Add ground chuck, Worcestershire sauce, salt and ¼ cup green onions. Mix only until combined. Spoon lightly into bottom and sides of 9-inch glass pie plate to form crust. Sprinkle remaining green onions over crust. Beat 3 eggs until foamy in same bowl. Stir in cheese, pepper sauce and ½ cup cream. Pour over green onions in crust. Sprinkle lightly with paprika. Microwave on High for 10 to 13 minutes, turning dish ¼ turn every 5 minutes. Let stand for 5 to 10-minutes before cutting into wedges. Yield: 6-8 servings.

Mildred Borden
Las Cruces, New Mexico

Beef Rarebit

1 lb. ground beef
½ c. chopped onion
¼ c. chopped green pepper
¾ c. beer
Dash of cayenne pepper
3 c. shredded Cheddar cheese
6 English muffins, split, toasted

Combine ground beef, onion and green pepper in glass bowl. Microwave on High for 5 to 6 minutes; drain. Add beer, cayenne pepper and cheese. Microwave on High for 3½ minutes longer. Pour over English muffins.

Sylvia Barton
Denver, Colorado

Crustless Pizza Pie

1 lb. extra lean ground beef
¼ c. chopped onion
⅓ c. quick-cooking oats
1 egg, beaten
½ tsp. salt
Dash of pepper
1 8-oz. can tomato sauce
1 tsp. leaf oregano
Green pepper rings
1 4-oz. can mushrooms, drained
½ c. shredded mozzarella cheese

Combine ground beef, onion, oats, egg, salt and pepper in mixing bowl. Combine tomato sauce and oregano; mix half the sauce into the meat mixture. Press into 9-inch glass pie plate. Arrange pepper rings in center. Cover with waxed paper. Microwave on High for 10 minutes or until beef is done. Drain off excess juices. Spoon remaining tomato sauce over top. Sprinkle with mushrooms and cheese. Microwave on High for 3 minutes longer.

Louise Albright
Tucson, Arizona

Spinach Lasagna

1 lb. ground beef
1 6-oz. can tomato sauce
¼ c. minced onion
1 tsp. sweet basil
1 tsp. parsley flakes
¼ tsp. oregano
Dash each of garlic salt, pepper
1 4-oz. can sliced mushrooms, drained
1 10-oz. package frozen chopped spinach
8 oz. cottage cheese
4 oz. mozzarella cheese, shredded

Crumble ground beef into glass casserole. Microwave on High for 6 minutes; drain. Stir in next 8 ingredients. Microwave spinach on High for 3 minutes to thaw; drain. Mix spinach and cottage cheese in bowl. Alternate layers of spinach mixture, ground beef and cheese in glass baking dish until all ingredients are used. Microwave on Medium for 12 minutes or until hot and bubbly. Yield: 4 servings.

Betty Mills
Buena Park, California

Traditional Lasagna

1 8-oz. package lasagne noodles
1 tsp. salt
1½ lb. ground beef
½ c. chopped onion
¼ c. chopped green pepper
1 pkg. spaghetti sauce mix
2 c. tomato sauce
½ c. drained mushroom pieces
1½ c. cottage cheese
6 to 8 oz. sliced mozzarella cheese
½ c. grated Parmesan cheese

Place noodles in 9 × 13-inch glass baking dish. Cover with water. Sprinkle with salt. Microwave on High, uncovered, for 15 minutes. Remove from oven. Let noodles stand in cooking water while preparing sauce. Crumble ground beef in 3-quart glass casserole. Add onion and green pepper. Microwave on High for 5 minutes, uncovered; stir well. Microwave for 3 minutes longer; drain off juices. Stir in spaghetti sauce mix, tomato sauce and mushrooms. Alternate layers of noodles, sauce, cottage cheese and mozzarella cheese in 9 ×

13-inch baking dish ending with noodles and sauce. Sprinkle with Parmesan cheese. Cover loosely with waxed paper. Microwave on High for 8 minutes; turn dish. Microwave for 7 minutes longer. Let stand for 5 minutes before serving.

Wilma Scott
Parsons, Kansas

Microwave Tortilla Casserole

6 flour tortillas, cut into 1-in. squares
Oil
2 to 3 c. shredded cooked roast beef
Salt to taste
½ c. sour cream
½ c. chopped green onions
1 c. grated Monterey Jack cheese
½ to 1 c. canned green chili salsa

Fry tortillas in hot oil in skillet until crisp; drain. Combine next 5 ingredients in bowl; mix well. Layer tortilla chips and meat mixture in glass casserole. Top with salsa. Microwave on High for 4 minutes. Garnish with guacamole and additional sour cream.

Carol Shaw
Chula Vista, California

Microwave Boeuf Bourguignon

1 to 1½ lb. beef round steak
3 tbsp. flour
2 tsp. instant beef bouillon
1 tbsp. onion flakes
½ tsp. salt
¼ tsp. pepper
⅓ c. cooking wine
1 onion, sliced
1 can mushrooms, drained

Cut steak into serving-sized pieces. Combine flour, instant bouillon, onion flakes, salt and pepper. Dredge steaks with flour mixture. Place in glass casserole. Add wine and ¼ cup water. Cover. Microwave on High for 3 minutes. Turn steaks. Microwave on High for 2 minutes or until no longer pink. Top with onion and mushrooms. Cover. Microwave on Low for 15 minutes or until tender.

Karen Kangas
Grand Rapids, Minnesota

Ham and Potato Bake

1 can cream of chicken soup
½ c. milk
Dash of pepper
4 c. sliced potatoes
1 c. diced cooked ham
1 sm. onion, sliced
1 tbsp. butter
Paprika to taste

Combine soup, milk and pepper in small mixing bowl; mix well. Layer potatoes, ham, onion and soup mixture in 8 × 8 × 2-inch glass baking dish. Dot with butter. Sprinkle with paprika. Microwave on High for 15 minutes.

Tammy Winslow
Huntsville, Alabama

Polynesian Ham

4 c. cooked rice
2 c. diced cooked ham
1 onion, sliced
1 tsp. dry mustard
½ tsp. salt
1 c. diced green pepper
1 20-oz. can pineapple chunks, drained
1 tbsp. brown sugar
¼ tsp. pepper

Combine rice, ham, onion, mustard and salt in 12 × 7-inch glass casserole; mix well. Top with green pepper and pineapple chunks. Sprinkle with brown sugar and pepper. Cover with waxed paper. Microwave on High for 10 to 15 minutes.

Andrea Freeman
Carmel, California

Apple and Sausage-Filled Crepes

½ lb. pork sausage
1 lb. apples, peeled, sliced
¼ c. raisins
2 tsp. cornstarch
Pancake syrup
½ tsp. ground cinnamon
Crepes

Place crumbled sausage between paper towels in Microwave. Microwave on High for 2 to 3 minutes or until sausage is cooked. Combine apples, raisins, cornstarch, 2 tablespoons pancake syrup and cinnamon in large glass bowl; mix well. Cover with waxed paper. Microwave on High for 3 to 5 minutes or until apples are tender and sauce thickens. Add sausage; mix well. Place ¼ cup of apple mixture down center of each crepe; roll up. Place filled crepes seam side down, in glass baking dish. Pour ¼ cup pancake syrup over crepes. Cover tightly with plastic wrap. Microwave on High for 3 to 4 minutes or until heated through.

Marjorie McPherson
Ames, Iowa

Cheesy Pork and Cabbage

1 to 1½-lb. boneless pork, cut into 1-in. cubes
1 can Cheddar cheese soup
4 med. carrots, shredded
2 tsp. brown sugar
1 tsp. salt
¼ tsp. caraway seed
Dash of pepper
1 tsp. vinegar
5 c. shredded cabbage

Place pork in 2½-quart glass casserole. Cover. Microwave on High for 8 to 10 minutes or until meat is no longer pink. Stir in soup, carrots, brown sugar, salt, caraway seed, pepper and vinegar. Cover. Microwave on High for 5 to 6 minutes or until mixture boils. Add cabbage. Cover. Microwave on High for 12 to 15 minutes or until pork and cabbage are tender, stirring every 5 minutes.

Myra Phelps
Greg Bull, Wyoming

Bavarian Smoked Pork Chops

2 c. drained sauerkraut
1 sm. onion, chopped
2 med. apples, chopped
1 tbsp. sugar
4 smoked pork chops

Combine sauerkraut, onion, apples and sugar in bowl; mix well. Spread half the sauerkraut mixture in 2-quart glass baking dish. Place pork chops over sauerkraut mixture. Cover with remaining sauerkraut mixture. Pour ½ cup water over top. Cover. Microwave on High for 5 minutes. Microwave on Defrost for 6 to 8 minutes or until apples are tender. Yield: 4 servings.

Sue Hepburn
San Diego, California

Italiano Chops

1 8-oz. can mushrooms, drained
1 c. chopped green pepper
1 med. onion, sliced
1 16-oz. can tomatoes, drained
1 tsp. each oregano salt
¼ tsp. pepper
½ tsp. garlic powder
4 pork chops

Combine all ingredients except pork chops in 3-quart glass casserole; mix well. Arrange pork chops on top; cover. Microwave on Roast for 20 to 25 minutes, turning pork chops halfway through cooking cycle.

Carla Dodge
Prescott, Arizona

Spanish Pork Chop Bake

1 15½-oz. jar spaghetti sauce
¾ c. long-grain rice
1½ tsp. instant chicken bouillon
¾ tsp. salt
Dash of pepper
½ c. sliced black olives
1 med. onion, sliced
6 pork loin chops

Combine spaghetti sauce, rice, bouillon, salt, pepper, olives, onion and 1⅔ cups water in 2-quart glass baking dish; mix well. Cover. Microwave on High for 5 minutes. Arrange pork chops on top; cover loosely. Microwave on High for 15 minutes. Turn and rearrange chops; stir rice. Cover tightly. Microwave on High for 10 to 15 minutes longer or until chops and rice are tender. Yield: 6 servings.

Cindy Longworth
Cedar Rapids, Iowa

Spicy Pork

1 16-oz. can tomatoes
1 med. onion, sliced
½ c. chopped celery
¼ c. chopped green pepper
1½ tsp. chili powder
1 tsp. salt

¼ tsp. pepper
4 pork chops

Combine first 7 ingredients with ½ cup water in 3-quart glass casserole; mix well. Arrange pork chops on top; cover. Microwave on Roast for 13 minutes; turn pork chops. Microwave on Roast for 13 minutes longer.

Annette Ellison
Louisville, Kentucky

Chili-Chicken Casserole

1 can cream of chicken soup
1 4-oz. can diced green chiles, drained
¼ tsp. instant minced onion
1 6-oz. package corn chips
2 5-oz. cans boned chicken, diced
2 lg. firm ripe tomatoes, peeled, sliced
1 c. shredded mild Cheddar cheese

Combine soup, chiles, onion and ½ cup water in small bowl; blend well. Alternate layers of corn chips, chicken tomato, soup mixture and cheese in 2-quart baking dish until all ingredients are used ending with cheese. Microwave on High for 15 minutes. Let stand for 5 minutes before serving.

Peggy O. Munter
Moore, Oklahoma

Microwave Chicken with Wild Rice

1 6-oz. package brown and wild rice mix
¼ lb. mushrooms, sliced
¼ c. dry Sherry
2 lb. chicken breasts and thighs
Paprika

Reserve 1 tablespoon rice seasoning mix. Combine remaining seasoning with rice, mushrooms, Sherry and 1⅓ cups hot water in 7 × 11-inch glass baking dish. Cover. Microwave on High for 15 minutes; stir rice. Season chicken pieces with reserved seasoning mix. Arrange chicken skin side up over rice. Sprinkle with paprika; cover. Microwave on High for 12 to 15 minutes or until chicken is no longer pink near bone, turning dish every 5 minutes. Let stand for 5 minutes.

Rochelle Vinson
Caldwell, Montana

Deanna's Chicken-Licken Chicken

1 2½ to 3-lb. chicken, cut up
¼ c. mayonnaise
½ c. bottled Russian dressing
1 pkg. dry onion soup mix
1 c. apricot-pineapple preserves

Arrange chicken pieces in 12 × 8-inch glass baking dish with thickest meaty pieces around edges of dish. Stir remaining ingredients together in bowl; blend well. Spread over chicken, coating each piece. Cover dish with paper towel or waxed paper. Microwave on High for 20 to 25 minutes or until tender.

Deanna L. Irwin
Phoenix, Arizona

Turkey-Spaghetti in a Microwave

2 tbsp. margarine
1 med. onion, finely chopped
1 clove of garlic, minced
1 1-lb. can tomatoes, chopped
1 can mushroom stems and pieces
1 tsp. salt
¼ tsp. pepper
¼ tsp. cayenne pepper
1½ c. diced cooked turkey
1 8-oz. package spaghetti, cooked
½ to 1 lb. Cheddar cheese, grated

Place margarine in 3-quart glass casserole; cover. Microwave on High for 1½ minutes or until melted. Add onion and garlic; cover. Microwave on High for 4 minutes. Stir in remaining ingredients except spaghetti and cheese; cover. Microwave on High for 8 to 10 minutes or until heated through, stirring once. Stir in spaghetti; top with cheese. Cover. Microwave on Medium for 4 to 6 minutes or until heated through.

Janet Morgan
Premont, Texas

California Vegetable Bake

1 pkg. frozen mixed vegetables
1 can Cheddar cheese soup

Combine all ingredients in glass casserole; mix well. Microwave on High for 12 to 15 minutes, stirring and turning occasionally.

Carol Zwolanek
Chippewa Falls, Wisconsin

Cheezy Broccoli-Rice Casserole

1 pkg. frozen chopped broccoli
1 tbsp. dried onion flakes
1 c. cooked rice
1 can cream of mushroom soup
Salt and pepper to taste
1 8-oz. jar Cheez Whiz

Place broccoli package in microwave. Microwave on High for 6 minutes. Combine broccoli with remaining ingredients except Cheez Whiz in glass casserole; mix well. Top with Cheez Whiz. Microwave on High for 10 minutes or until bubbly. Yield: 6 servings.

Rowena Reed
College Station, Texas

Broccoli in Chicken-Dill Sauce

1 lb. fresh broccoli
2 tbsp. margarine
¼ c. chopped onion
1 can cream of chicken soup
⅔ c. milk
¼ tsp. dried dillweed
Dash of pepper

Cut broccoli into serving-sized pieces, removing tough stem ends. Place in 2-quart glass casserole with ¼ cup water. Cover with waxed paper. Microwave on high for 8 to 10 minutes, or until tender; drain well. Place margarine and onion in glass bowl. Cover with waxed paper. Microwave on High for 2 minutes or until onion is tender. Stir in soup, milk, dillweed and pepper. Pour over broccoli. Microwave on High, uncovered, for 4 minutes longer. Yield: 6 servings.

Ruby Taylor
Cleveland, Tennessee

Barbara's Microwave Broccoli

1 pkg. frozen broccoli
1 c. grated American cheese
1 can cream of mushroom soup
⅓ c. evaporated milk
1 can onion rings

Place broccoli in greased 2-quart glass casserole. Microwave on High, covered, for 5 to 6 minutes, stirring once; drain. Sprinkle with cheese. Blend soup and milk in bowl; pour over broccoli. Microwave on Medium for 6 minutes. Top with onion rings. Microwave on High for 2½ minutes. Yield: 4 servings.

Barbara Smoot
Selma, Indiana

Microwave Scalloped Potatoes

4 c. sliced potatoes
¼ c. chopped onion
¾ tsp. salt
⅛ tsp. pepper
1 can cream of celery soup
½ c. milk
Paprika

Alternate layers of potatoes and onion in greased 2-quart casserole until all ingredients are used. Blend next 4 ingredients in bowl. Pour over potatoes. Cover. Microwave on High for 20 minutes, stirring every 5 minutes. Sprinkle with paprika. Let stand for 5 minutes before serving.

Pamela Vaughn
Clarksville, Texas

Potatoes Au Gratin

½ c. chopped green onions
1 tbsp. butter
Dash of pepper
1 can chicken gravy
¾ c. milk
4 c. thinly sliced potatoes
1 c. shredded sharp Cheddar cheese
Paprika

Combine onions, butter and pepper in 1-quart glass measuring cup. Microwave on High for 1 minute. Stir in gravy and milk. Alternate layers of potatoes, gravy mixture and cheese in 1½-quart glass casserole. Sprinkle with paprika. Cover. Microwave on High for 35 minutes or until tender.

DeVonna M. Hyde
Welcome, Minnesota

Spring Vegetable Medley

2 tbps. butter
½ lb. fresh asparagus cut in 2-inch pieces
½ tsp. basil
⅛ tsp. pepper
½ lb. fresh mushrooms, sliced
1 med. tomato, cut in wedges
½ tsp. salt

Microwave butter in 1½-quart glass casserole for 30 seconds or until melted. Combine asparagus, basil and pepper in casserole; mix well. Microwave, covered, on High for 3 minutes. Add mushrooms; mix well. Microwave, covered, on High for 3 minutes. Add tomato; mix well. Microwave, covered, on High for 1½ minutes. Stir in salt. Let stand, covered, for 3 minutes before serving.

Picture for this recipe on page 99.

Ann's Crock•Pot Chili

2 lb. boneless beef round steak
1 c. chopped onion
2 c. chopped celery
½ c. chopped green pepper
1 1-lb. 13-oz. can tomatoes, blended
3 tbsp. Worcestershire sauce
2 tsp. each salt, paprika, chili
1 tsp. each garlic powder, cumin
1 can red kidney beans, drained
1 can garbanzo beans, drained
3 tbsp. lemon juice
¼ c. chopped parsley

Combine all ingredients except beans, lemon juice and parsley in Crock•Pot; cover. Cook on Low for 6 hours. Add beans; cover. Cook on High for 1 hour longer. Stir in lemon juice and parsley; serve immediately. Yield: 8-10 servings.

Ann Morris
Basalt, Colorado

Crock•Pot Stew

1 lb. stew beef
1 lb. ham, chopped
2 tbsp. shortening
2 tsp. salt
2 lg. onions, cubed
2 c. sliced carrots
2 c. chopped potatoes
2 c. chopped rutabagas
1 c. sliced celery

Brown stew beef and ham slowly in shortening in skillet; drain. Place in Crock•Pot with remaining ingredients. Add water to cover. Cook on High for 4 hours or until meat is tender.

Eleanor Edwards
Kent Washington

Crocked Beef Deluxe

3 to 4 peeled potatoes, quartered
4 to 6 onions, halved
1 3 to 6-lb. beef chuck roast
Salt and pepper to taste
1 can tomato soup
1 4-oz. can mushroom stems and pieces

Place potatoes and onions in Crock•Pot. Add roast, salt and pepper. Pour soup and 1 cup water over top. Arrange mushrooms over top; cover. Cook on Low for 8 to 10 hours or for 4 to 6 hours on High.

Fleeta Pendleton
Raliegh, North Carolina

Four-Hour Stew

6 to 8 med. potatoes, cubed
2 c. celery, cut into 1-in. pieces
14 carrots, cut into 1-in. pieces
8 med. onions
½ green pepper, chopped
4 to 5 lb. beef stew meat, cubed
1 tbsp. salt
Pepper to taste
3 tbsp. sugar
6 tbsp. Minute tapioca
1 28-oz. can tomatoes
1 can peas, drained

Place first 6 ingredients in Crock•Pot. Sprinkle with salt and pepper. Combine next 3 ingredients in bowl; mix well. Pour into Crock•Pot. Cook on High for 4 hours or until beef is tender. Stir in peas. Cook for ½ hour longer. Yield: 10-12 servings.

Jan Welson
Appleton, Wisconsin

Crock•Pot Herbed Steak

1 2-lb. beef round steak, trimmed
Flour
½ tsp. salt
⅛ tsp. pepper
2 tbsp. cooking oil
1 med. onion, sliced
1 can cream of celery soup
½ tsp. dried oregano
¼ tsp. dried thyme, crushed

Cut steak into 6 serving pieces. Coat in flour seasoned with salt and pepper. Pound on both sides. Brown in oil in skillet; drain, reserving 1 tablespoon drippings. Place steak in Crock•Pot. Saute onion in reserved drippings. Stir in remaining ingredients except flour. Spoon over steak. Cook, covered, on Low setting for 8 to 10 hours. Remove steak to heated platter. Pour juices into saucepan. Blend ⅓ cup water and 3 tablespoons flour. Stir into liquid. Cook until thick, stirring constantly. Pour over steaks. Yield: 6 servings.

Sheila Turnage
Hayti, Missouri

Slow Cooker Beef and Beans

1 lb. dried pinto beans
½ lb. salt pork, cut up
1 lb. lean beef chuck steak, cubed
1 red chili pepper
1 med. onion, chopped
2 cloves of garlic, minced
1 6-oz. can tomato paste
2 tsp. each chili powder, salt
1 tsp. cumin seed
½ tsp. marjoram leaves

Soak beans in 6 cups cold water overnight. Brown salt pork in skillet. Combine all ingredients in slow cooker; cover. Cook on Low for 9 to 10 hours. Yield: 8 servings.

Dena Silvers
Decatur, Texas

Spicy Beef Stew

2 lb. stew meat
1 lg. can tomatoes
8 carrots, cut in lg. chunks
1 c. celery chunks
½ pkg. onion soup mix
1 tbsp. sugar
1 tbsp. salt
½ c. cooking Sherry
3 tbsp. tapioca
2 slices bread, cubed
Dash of marjoram
Dash of rosemary
Dash of thyme
1 pkg. frozen peas, cooked

Combine all ingredients except peas in Crock•Pot. Cook, covered, on high setting for 5 hours. Add peas. Cook 1 hour longer or until tender. Yield: 6-8 servings.

Mary Cay Ross
Mahtomedi, Minnesota

Super Beef Supper

3 lbs. beef brisket
3 cabbage leaves, chopped fine
Salt to taste
1 can tomato paste
1 c. chopped celery
1 lg. marrow bone
5 carrots, diced fine
1 med. onion, chopped
⅛ tsp. pepper
½ c. pearl barley
¼ c. chopped parsley

Combine all ingredients with 4 cups water in slow cooker. Cook on High for 5 hours or until beef is tender.

Barre Line
Belt, Montana

Corned Beef and Cabbage in a Crock•Pot

1 4-lb. corned beef
4 carrots
2 onions, halved
4 peppercorns
3 potatoes, quartered
½ cabbage, halved

Soak corned beef in water overnight. Place beef in slow cooker with 2½ cups water, carrots, onions and peppercorns. Cover. Cook on Low for 8 hours. Add potatoes and cabbage. Cook on Low for 4 to 6 hours longer or on High for 2 to 3 hours.

Peggy Bupp
Smithville, Ohio

Calico Beans

½ lb. bacon
1 lb. ground beef
½ c. chopped onions
1 16-oz. can pork and beans
1 16-oz. can kidney beans
1 16-oz. can lima beans, drained
½ c. packed brown sugar
½ c. catsup
⅓ tsp. salt
1 tsp. dry mustard
2 tsp. vinegar

Cook bacon until crisp; drain and reserve drippings. Crumble bacon; set aside. Cook ground beef and onions in bacon drippings until lightly browned. Add bacon and beef mixture to Crock•Pot. Add pork and beans, kidney beans and lima beans. Combine remaining ingredients in bowl; stir into bean mixture. Cook on Low for 6 to 8 hours.

Adeline Brill
Jamestown, New York

Pinto Chili

½ lb. dried pinto beans
2 1-lb. cans tomatoes
1 lb. lean ground beef, browned
2 med. onions, coarsely chopped
1 green onion, coarsely chopped
2 cloves of garlic, crushed
⅔ tbsp. chili powder
1½ tsp. salt
1 tsp. pepper
1 tsp. apple cider vinegar (opt.)

Soak beans in water overnight; drain. Place all ingredients in Crock•Pot. Put in order listed with 2 cups water. Stir once. Cover. Cook on Low for 10 to 12 hours or on High for 5 to 6 hours.

Catherine G. Ward
Forest Park, Georgia

Hawaiian Ribs in a Crock•Pot

2 tbsp. cornstarch
3 tbsp. brown sugar
½ tsp. salt
¼ c. vinegar
½ c. catsup
1 tbsp. soy sauce
1 9-oz. can crushed pineapple
3 lb. spareribs, trimmed

Combine all ingredients except spareribs in saucepan. Bring to a boil. Cook until thick, stirring frequently. Arrange sauce and spareribs in layers in Crock•Pot. Cover. Cook on low setting for 6 to 8 hours or until tender. Yield: 6 servings.

Betty Rassette
Salina, Kansas

Slow Italian Pork Chops

6 pork chops
2 cans French-cut green beans
2 8-oz. cans tomato sauce
½ c. chopped green pepper
1 clove of garlic, chopped
1 med. onion, chopped

Brown pork chops in skillet. Place remaining ingredients in slow cooker; add pork chops and water to cover. Cook on Low for 6 to 8 hours.

Peggy Bupp
Smithville, Ohio

Crock•Pot Brunswick Stew

1 5-lb. hen
1 No. 2 can tomatoes
1 8-oz. can tomato paste
1 No. 2 can okra
1 No. 2 can corn
2 lb. potatoes
2 lg. onions
Red pepper and salt to taste

Place hen in Crock•Pot with water to cover. Cook on High 2 to 3 hours until very tender. Remove chicken; debone. Chop chicken; return to Crock•Pot. Add remaining ingredients. Cook on High for 4 hours. Yield: 12 servings.

Missie Henry
Canton, Mississippi

Crock•Pot Chicken and Rice

¾ c. rice
1 can cream of celery soup
1 can cream of mushroom soup
1 c. white wine
1 sm. can whole mushrooms
1 sm. jar pimento strips, drained
½ green pepper, chopped
½ onion, chopped
1 can water chestnuts, drained, sliced
8 to 12 chicken breast halves
Grated Parmesan cheese

Place rice in Crock•Pot. Combine remaining ingredients except chicken and cheese in bowl; mix well. Pour ⅓ mixture over rice. Place chicken on top. Pour remaining soup mixture over all. Cook on High for 3 hours or until chicken is tender. Garnish with cheese.

Laurie Phillips
Ellyn, Illinois

Crock•Pot Lemon-Chicken

¼ c. flour
1¼ tsp. salt
2 2½ to 3-lb. fryers, cut up
2 tbsp. oil
1 6-oz. can frozen lemonade, thawed
3 tbsp. brown sugar
3 tbsp. catsup
1 tbsp. vinegar
2 tbsp. cornstarch

Coat chicken with flour seasoned with salt. Saute chicken on all sides in oil in skillet until brown; drain. Place in Crock•Pot. Stir lemonade concentrate, brown sugar, catsup and vinegar together in bowl; pour over chicken. Cover. Cook on High for 3 to 4 hours. Remove chicken; pour liquid into saucepan. Return chicken to Crock•Pot; cover to keep warm. Skim fat from liquid. Blend 2 tablespoons cold water slowly into cornstarch; stir into hot liquid. Cook until thickened and bubbly, stirring constantly. Serve chicken with gravy over hot cooked rice. Yield: 6 servings.

Gloria Haiwick
Highmore, South Dakota

Pepper Chicken

1 2½ to 3-lb. fryer, cut up
¼ c. soy sauce
½ tsp. salt
1 8½-oz. can water chestnuts, drained, sliced
1 green pepper, cut into 1-in. pieces
2 tsp. cornstarch

Remove skin and fat from chicken. Place in Crock•Pot. Combine soy sauce and salt with 1 tablespoon water. Pour over chicken. Cook, covered, for 1½ hours. Add water chestnuts and green pepper. Cook for ½ hour longer. Combine cornstarch and 2 tablespoons water. Stir into liquid in Crock•Pot. Cook until thick, stirring constantly. Yield: 6 servings.

Evelyn Knowles
Wilson, North Carolina

Susan's Crock•Pot Chicken

2 to 3 carrots, sliced
2 to 3 stalks celery, cut in pieces
1 med. onion, halved
1 tbsp. chopped dried onion tops (opt.)
1 tbsp. minced parsley
1 chicken bouillon cube
1 3-lb. chicken

Place carrots, celery and onion halves in Crock•Pot. Sprinkle in onion tops and parsley; add bouillon cube. Place whole chicken on top of vegetables; pour 1 cup water over chicken. Cover. Cook on Low for 8 hours or until chicken is tender.

Susan K. Dreier
New Wilmington, Pennsylvania

Easy Venison Roast

½ c. vinegar
1 3 to 4-lb. venison roast
Salt
1 tsp. lemon-pepper marinade
½ tsp. oregano
1 tsp. seasoned salt
3 cloves of garlic, quartered
1 sm. onion, chopped

Combine vinegar and 2 quarts water. Add roast; soak overnight. Rinse well. Soak in salted water for 2 hours; rinse. Combine 1 teaspoon salt, lemon-pepper marinade, oregano and seasoned salt; rub on roast. Cover with garlic and onion. Place in a slow cooker. Add ¼ to ⅓ cup water. Cook on Low setting for 6 to 8 hours.

Carol V. McClelland
Meadville, Mississippi

Great Bean Bake

4 c. dried beans
½ c. diced bacon
1 sm. onion, chopped
¼ c. packed brown sugar
¼ c. molasses
1 tsp. prepared mustard
4 tbsp. catsup
1 tsp. salt

Soak beans overnight. Drain well. Combine beans with remaining ingredients in Crock•Pot.

Cover beans with water. Cook on High until water boils. Turn to Low. Cook for 5 hours longer. Yield: 12 servings.

Jeanette B. Kramer
Rice Lake, Wisconsin

Border-Style Bean Soup

3 c. dried pinto beans
1 lb. ground beef
1 tbsp. cooking oil
1 med. onion
1 lg. clove of garlic
1 tbsp. chili powder
1 tbsp. dried parsley
1 tbsp. dried celery
1 can tomatoes
2 carrots
Salt and pepper to taste

Wash beans; place in Crock•Pot with water to cover. Cook on High for 1 hour. Saute ground beef with onions and garlic in oil in skillet until crumbly. Add chili powder; mix well. Add ground beef and remaining ingredients to Crock•Pot. Cook for 3 hours longer or until beans are tender. Yield: 12 servings.

Katy Rick
Brownsville, Texas

Crock•Pot Cabbage Soup

1 sm. head cabbage, thinly sliced
2 c. frozen French-style green beans
½ c. chopped onions
4 to 6 stalks celery, diced
1 46-oz. can tomato juice
Salt and pepper to taste
4 beef bouillon cubes
6 tbsp. lemon juice
Chopped parsley to taste (opt.)
Chopped bell pepper to taste (opt.)
Chopped spinach to taste (opt.)

Combine all ingredients and 2 cups water in Crock•Pot. Cook on Low for about 8 hours or overnight.

Mary W. Hull
Pickens, South Carolina

Creamy Bean Soup

1 lb. dried navy beans
½ lb. bacon, crisp fried, crumbled
2 ham hocks
1 onion, minced
2 cloves of garlic, minced
1 stalk celery, minced
2 tbsp. dried parsley
Salt and pepper to taste
1 c. half and half

Soak beans overnight in water to cover; drain. Combine all ingredients with 5 cups water in Crock•Pot. Cook on low for 8 to 10 hours.

Linda Owens
Mount Vernon, Texas

Slow Vegetable Soup

4 beef prime rib bones
1 No. 303 can mixed vegetables
1 No. 303 can green beans
1 8-oz. can tomato sauce
½ c. diced mushrooms
½ onion, diced
½ tsp. sweet basil
1 tsp. chives
1 tbsp. chopped parsley
1 tsp. salt
½ tsp. pepper
1 c. noodles

Trim fat from bones. Drain mixed vegetables and green beans; reserve liquid. Combine tomato sauce, reserved liquid and enough water to measure 6 cups; pour into Crock•Pot. Add beef bones; cover. Cook on Low for 4 to 6 hours or until meat falls from bones. Remove bones. Stir in vegetables, herbs, seasonings and noodles; cover. Cook on Low for 2 to 3 hours longer or until noodles are tender. Yield: 10 servings.

Alice Jean Baker
San Francisco, California

Vegetable Soup in a Crock•Pot

1 lg. soupbone
¼ c. minced onion
1 c. minced celery leaves
2 bouillon cubes
½ tsp. salt
2 potatoes, diced
3 carrots, sliced
2 parsnips, sliced (opt.)
1 can mixed vegetables
¼ c. pearl barley

Place soupbone, 3 cups water, onion, celery leaves, bouillon and salt in Crock•Pot. Cook on Low overnight. Remove meat from bone; chop. Return to Crock•Pot. Add remaining vegetables and barley. Cook for 6 to 8 hours longer or until vegetables are tender.

Vicki Zoellner
Elkton, South Dakota

Crock•Pot Apple Cobbler

Oil
4 med. tart apples
½ c. sugar
Grated rind and juice of 1 lemon
Dash of cinnamon
5 tbsp. butter
¾ c. natural cereal with nuts and fruits

Grease side of 3½-quart Crock•Pot lightly with oil. Core, peel and slice apples; place in Crock•Pot. Add sugar, lemon rind, lemon juice and cinnamon. Combine butter and cereal. Add to Crock•Pot; mix thoroughly. Cover. Cook on Low for 6 to 8 hours or High for 2 to 3 hours. Serve with vanilla ice cream or whipped topping, if desired.

Mrs. Elizabeth B. Lengle
Turbotville, Pennsylvania

Crocked Fruit Compote

1 lb. dried prunes
1⅓ c. dried apricots
1⅔ c. pineapple chunks and juice
1 1-lb. can pitted dark sweet cherries
      and juice
¼ c. dry white wine

Combine all ingredients in Crock•Pot with 2 cups water; cover. Cook on Low for 7 to 8 hours or on High for 3 to 4 hours. Serve warm.

Mary Ellen Harrington
Worcester, Massachusetts

Desserts

Autumn Fruit Casserole

1 1-lb. can pineapple chunks
1 1-lb. 14-oz. can peach halves
1 1-lb. 4-oz. can apricot halves
⅓ c. melted butter
⅔ c. packed brown sugar
¼ tsp. each ground cloves, cinnamon
1 tbsp. curry powder

Drain all fruits well. Arrange in layers in medium casserole. Combine butter, sugar and spices in small bowl; mix until crumbly. Sprinkle over fruits. Bake in 350-degree oven for 1 hour. Serve hot with sour cream.

Elizabeth Peterson
Paullina, Iowa

Baked Apples

1 c. prunes
½ c. orange juice
4 med. baking apples, cored
½ c. packed brown sugar
¼ c. lemon juice
¼ c. red cinnamon candies

Combine prunes, ½ cup water and orange juice in saucepan. Bring to a boil. Boil for 15 minutes; drain. Pit prunes. Place 4 prunes in center of each apple. Spoon 2 teaspoons brown sugar and 1 teaspoon lemon juice into each apple; top with 1 teaspoon candies. Place apples in ungreased 8-inch cake pan. Bake at 350 degrees for 30 to 35 minutes or until apples are tender. Serve warm with vanilla ice cream.

Faith A. McCarn
Port Orchard, Wash.

Linda's Apple Casserole

4 or 5 med. baking apples, peeled, sliced
1 sm. can crushed pineapple
¼ c. red cinnamon candies
Flour
¾ c. sugar
5 tbsp. melted butter

Combine first 3 ingredients with 2 tablespoons flour in bowl; toss to mix. Spoon into greased 1½-quart casserole. Combine sugar and butter with ¾ cup flour in small bowl; mix well. Spread over apple mixture. Bake at 350 degrees for 30 minutes or until brown.

Linda Adams
Millersburg, Pennsylvania

Apple Cobbler

5 c. sliced apples
1¼ c. sugar
Flour
½ tsp. cinnamon
½ tsp. salt
1 tsp. vanilla extract
1 tbsp. butter
½ tsp. baking powder
2 tbsp. butter, softened
1 egg, slightly beaten

Combine apples, ¾ cup sugar, 2 tablespoons flour, cinnamon, ¼ teaspoon salt and vanilla in bowl. Add ¼ cup water; mix well. Pour into 9-inch square baking dish; dot with butter. Combine ½ cup sifted flour, remaining ½ cup sugar, baking powder, remaining salt, butter and egg in bowl. Beat until smooth. Drop batter in 9 portions over apples, spacing evenly. Bake in 375-degree oven for 35 to 40 minutes or until apples are fork-tender and crust is golden brown. Serve warm with whipped cream or ice cream.

Deborah Wheeler
Cabot, Vermont

Apple Crisp

4 c. pared sliced baking apples
⅔ to ¾ c. packed brown sugar
½ c. sifted flour
½ c. rolled oats
¾ tsp. each cinnamon, nutmeg
⅓ c. soft butter

Place apples in greased 8-inch square baking dish. Blend remaining ingredients in bowl until crumbly; spread over apples. Bake at 375 degrees for 30 to 35 minutes or until apples are tender and topping is golden brown. Serve warm with cream, ice cream or hard sauce. Yield: 6-8 servings.

Mildred J. Wallis
British Columbia, Canada

Apple Dumpling Pudding

2 c. chopped apples
½ c. melted shortening
1 c. sugar
1½ c. flour
1 egg, beaten
2 tsp. nutmeg

1 tsp. each cinnamon, soda
½ tsp. vanilla extract
Pinch of salt

Combine all ingredients in large bowl; mix well. Pour into baking dish. Bake at 375 degrees for 30 to 35 minutes.

Betty Jan Anderson
Savannah, Georgia

Applesauce Cobbler

1 can applesauce
1 box yellow cake mix
½ c. packed brown sugar
½ c. finely chopped pecans
2 sticks margarine, sliced

Spread applesauce in 9 × 9-inch baking dish. Sprinkle with cake mix. Top with brown sugar and pecans. Cover with margarine. Bake at 300 degrees for 1 hour. Yield: 8-10 servings.

Lois G. Salter
Zwolle, Louisiana

Applesauce Crisp

1 No. 2½ can applesauce
¼ c. crushed pineapple
½ stick butter, melted
1 c. quick-cooking oats
½ c. packed brown sugar
½ tsp. cinnamon (opt.)
½ tsp. salt

Combine applesauce and pineapple in 8-inch baking dish. Combine remaining ingredients in bowl; mix until crumbly. Sprinkle over fruit. Bake at 400 degrees for 20 minutes. Garnish with chopped pecans.

Ruby C. Goforth
Kershaw, S. C.

Wheat Germ-Apple Crisp

6 c. peeled, sliced cooking apples
⅔ c. packed brown sugar
½ c. flour
⅓ c. toasted wheat germ
6 tbsp. corn oil margarine

Place apple slices in shallow greased 1½-quart casserole. Mix remaining ingredients in bowl until crumbly. Sprinkle over apples. Bake at 375 degrees for 45 minutes or until apples are tender. Yield: 6 servings.

Geraldine Seedonff
Grand Meadow, Minnesota

Apricot Betty

1 c. bread crumbs
¼ c. packed brown sugar
¼ c. margarine, melted
½ tsp. each mace, cinnamon
¼ tsp. ginger
¼ c. nonfat dry milk
3 c. canned apricot halves, drained

Blend first 7 ingredients in bowl. Arrange apricots in baking dish. Sprinkle with crumb mixture. Bake for 30 minutes at 375 degrees. Serve warm with milk. Yield: 4-6 servings.

Deborah Purvis
Soquel, California

Baked Apricot Whip

¾ c. cooked dried apricots, pureed
4 egg whites, stiffly beaten
Dash of salt
3 tbsp. honey

Fold apricot puree into egg whites. Add salt and honey; mix lightly. Spoon into 1-quart casserole. Bake at 375 degrees for 30 minutes or until firm. Yield: 6 servings.

Elizabeth Trennepohl
Angola, Indiana

Blueberry Crumb Pudding

1 c. zwieback crumbs
¼ c. sugar
¼ tsp. cinnamon
3 tbsp. butter, melted
2 pkg. frozen blueberries, thawed

Combine first 4 ingredients in bowl; mix well. Alternate layers of blueberries and crumb mixture in 1-quart baking dish ending with crumbs. Bake at 350 degrees for 30 minutes. Yield: 4 servings.

Virginia Sheely
Littlestown, Pennsylvania

Blackberry Buckle

½ c. butter, softened
1 c. sugar
1 egg, well-beaten
1⅓ c. flour
1½ tsp. baking powder
⅛ tsp. salt
⅓ c. milk
1 tsp. vanilla extract
2 c. sweetened fresh blackberries
½ tsp. cinnamon

Cream ¼ cup butter, and ½ cup sugar together in bowl. Add egg; beat well. Sift 1 cup flour, baking powder and salt together. Add to creamed mixture alternately with milk and vanilla, beating well after each addition. Pour into greased and floured baking dish. Cover with blackberries. Cream remaining ¼ cup butter and ½ cup sugar in small bowl. Stir in ⅓ cup flour and cinnamon until crumbly. Sprinkle over blackberries. Bake at 375 degrees for 45 minutes or until brown.

Agnes C. Huffman
Modesto, California

Cherry Cobbler

1 can cherry pie filling
1 8-oz. can crushed pineapple, drained
1 pkg. yellow cake mix
Butter (opt.)

Mix pie filling and pineapple in 9 × 13-inch baking dish. Top with dry cake mix. Sprinkle with ½ cup warm water. Do not stir. Dot with butter. Bake at 350 degrees for 45 to 50 minutes or until brown. Yield: 6 servings.

Phyllis L. Barton
Alexandria, Virginia

Cherry Crumble

1 or 2 No. 303 cans tart pitted cherries
2 c. flour
1¼ tsp. salt
1¼ c. sugar
1 c. melted butter
Cinnamon to taste
Cloves to taste

Drain cherries, reserving juice. Mix next 4 ingredients in bowl until crumbly. Place half the crumb mixture in 9-inch square pan. Spoon cherries over top. Sprinkle with cinnamon and cloves. Pat remaining crumb mixture on top. Sprinkle with cinnamon and cloves. Bake at 375 degrees for 30 to 40 minutes or until golden brown.

Karen Doerksen
Colorado Springs, Colorado

Cherry Crunch

1 can cherry pie filling
1 tsp. lemon juice
1 pkg. cherry supreme cake mix
½ c. nuts
½ c. margarine, melted

Spread pie filling in 9 × 9-inch baking dish. Sprinkle with lemon juice. Combine remaining ingredients in bowl; mix until crumbly. Spread over pie filling. Bake at 350 degrees for 45 to 50 minutes or until brown. Yield: 8-10 servings.

Linda Medlen
Tiptonville, Tennessee

Cherry-Orange Rolls

1 can cherry pie filling
1 pkg. refrigerated orange Danish rolls

Spread pie filling in buttered 9-inch cake pan. Arrange rolls over filling. Bake at 350 degrees for 30 minutes or until brown. Frost rolls, using package directions.

Janis Williams
New London, Texas

Cherry Pudding

1 tbsp. butter, melted
1 c. flour
½ c. milk
1 tsp. baking powder
1¾ c. sugar
2 c. canned cherries

Combine first four ingredients with 1 cup sugar in bowl. Beat until smooth. Pour into baking dish. Heat cherries and remaining ¾ cup sugar in saucepan until sugar dissolves. Pour over batter. Bake at 375 degrees for 25 minutes or until brown. Yield: 9 servings.

Ella Mae Broyles
Edmond, Oklahoma

Quick Fruit Casserole

2 sticks pie crust mix, crumbled
½ c. sugar
¼ tsp. cinnamon
¼ tsp. nutmeg
1 can cherry pie filling

Combine first 4 ingredients in small bowl; mix well. Pour pie filling into greased 8 × 8-inch baking dish. Spread topping over filling. Bake at 375 degrees for 20 minutes or until brown.

Helen Cade
Thomaston, Alabama

Healthy Dessert Casserole

2 c. flour
2 c. sugar
1 tsp. each soda, cinnamon, cloves
¼ tsp. salt
⅔ c. shortening
2 c. chopped apples
2 c. grated carrots
1 c. raisins
½ c. nuts

Sift dry ingredients into bowl. Cut in shortening until crumbly. Stir in remaining ingredients; mix well. Place in 8 × 12-inch baking dish. Bake at 350 degrees for 30 minutes. Garnish with coconut.

Allyene Gregory
Owensboro, Kentucky

Hot Fruit Compote

12 dried macaroons, crumbled
4 c. mixed drained fruits
½ c. slivered toasted almonds
½ c. packed brown sugar
½ c. Sherry
¼ c. melted butter

Cover bottom of buttered 2½-quart casserole with layer of macaroon crumbs. Alternate layers of fruits and crumbs, ending with crumbs. Sprinkle with almonds, brown sugar and Sherry. Bake at 350 degrees for 30 minutes. Add butter. Serve hot. Yield: 6-8 servings.

Mrs. S. C. Young
Pine Bluff, Arkansas

Baked Devil's Float

1 c. sugar
12 marshmallows, quartered
2 tbsp. shortening
1 tsp. vanilla extract
1 c. flour
½ tsp. salt
1 tsp. baking powder
3 tbsp. cocoa
½ c. milk
½ c. chopped nuts

Combine ½ cup sugar and 1½ cups water in saucepan. Bring to a boil. Cook for 5 minutes. Pour into baking dish. Top with marshmallows. Cream shortening and ½ cup sugar in bowl. Add vanilla. Sift dry ingredients together. Add to creamed mixture alternately with milk beating well after each addition. Add nuts. Drop by spoonfuls over marshmallows. Cover. Bake at 350 degrees for 45 minutes. Yield: 6 servings.

Gladys Frye
Chilhowie, Virginia

Chocolate Dumplings

Sugar
Salt
1 sq. chocolate
¼ c. shortening
1 tsp. cinnamon
2 sq. chocolate, melted
1 c. flour
2 tsp. baking powder
½ tsp. soda
⅔ c. milk

Combine ⅔ cup sugar, ⅛ teaspoon salt, 1 square chocolate and 2 cups water in saucepan. Bring to a boil, stirring to blend chocolate. Pour into casserole. Cream shortening, ½ teaspoon salt, cinnamon and ¼ cup sugar in bowl. Add melted chocolate; blend well. Sift dry ingredients. Add to creamed mixture alternately with milk, beating well after each addition. Drop by spoonfuls on hot syrup. Bake at 350 degrees for 45 minutes.

Ruby Bundy
Lida, Kentucky

Chocolate Bread Pudding

4 slices dry bread
1 sq. unsweetened chocolate, chopped
4 c. milk
2 eggs, beaten
1 c. sugar
1 tsp. vanilla extract

Remove bread crusts; crumble bread. Combine bread crumbs, chocolate and milk in saucepan. Heat to scalding, stirring occasionally. Beat eggs and sugar in large bowl. Pour milk mixture over eggs slowly, stirring constantly. Stir in vanilla. Pour into large casserole. Place in pan of hot water. Bake at 350 degrees for 1 hour or until knife inserted in center comes out clean.

Barbara A. Crosby
Westbury, N. Y.

Chocolate Pudding

1 c. flour
¼ tsp. salt
1½ c. sugar
2 tsp. baking powder
4½ tbsp. cocoa
½ c. milk
2 tbsp. melted butter
1 tsp. vanilla extract
½ c. chopped pecans

Sift flour, salt, ¾ cup sugar, baking powder, and 1½ tablespoons cocoa together in bowl. Add milk, butter, vanilla and nuts; mix well. Pour into 9-inch baking pan. Cover with remaining ¾ cup sugar, 3 tablespoons cocoa and 1 cup water. Do not stir. Bake at 325 degrees until cake crust tests done. Serve warm.

Jane Kiker
Allison, Texas

Fudge Marble Pudding

1 sm. box white cake mix
½ c. sugar
5 tbsp. cocoa
⅛ tsp. salt

Prepare cake mix using package directions. Combine remaining ingredients with 1⅔ cup boiling water in bowl; mix well. Pour into 10 × 6-inch baking dish. Spoon batter over top. Bake at 350 degrees for 40 to 45 minutes.

Agnes Smithwich
Roanoke Rapids, Virginia

Lemon-Coconut Cups

1 c. sugar
¼ c. sifted flour
Dash of salt
2 tbsp. melted butter
2 tbsp. grated lemon peel
⅓ c. lemon juice
1½ c. milk, scalded
3 eggs, separated
½ c. shredded coconut

Combine first 6 ingredients in bowl; mix well. Add milk into beaten egg yolks slowly, stirring constantly. Blend egg yolk mixture into sugar mixture. Beat egg whites until stiff peaks form. Fold egg whites and coconut into sugar mixture. Fill custard cups ⅔ full. Place in shallow pan in 1-inch of hot water. Bake at 325 degrees for 45 minutes or until cake layer on top tests done. Yield: 6-8 servings.

Caroline Timberlake
Kensington, Maryland

Lemon Delicious

2 tbsp. butter, softened
¾ c. sugar
2 eggs, separated
1 lemon, juice and grated rind
1 tbsp. flour
1 c. milk
⅛ tsp. salt

Cream butter and sugar together in bowl. Add well-beaten egg yolks, lemon juice, lemon rind and flour; beat well. Beat in milk and salt. Beat egg whites until stiff peaks form. Fold into batter. Pour into baking dish. Place in pan with 1-inch hot water. Bake at 350 degrees for 30 to 40 minutes or until knife inserted in center comes out clean. Yield: 4 servings.

Sammy Saulsbury
Odessa, Texas

Magic Orange Cups

¾ c. sugar
1½ tbsp. shortening
1 tbsp. grated orange rind
2 eggs, separated
3 tbsp. flour
⅓ c. orange juice
1 c. (scant) milk

Cream sugar and shortening in bowl. Add orange peel and beaten yolks; beat well. Add flour alternately with milk and juice, beating well after each addition. Beat egg whites until stiff peaks form. Fold into batter. Spoon into greased custard cups. Place in pan in 1-inch hot water. Bake at 350 degrees for 20 minutes.

Willa Dailey
Gibbon, Nebraska

Mixed Fruit Casserole

¼ c. melted butter
3 tbsp. flour
½ tsp. curry powder
1 13-oz. can peach halves
1 1-lb. 4-oz. can pineapple spears
1 1-lb. can pears
1 1-lb. can whole apricots
1 stick of whole ginger
¼ c. packed brown sugar

Combine first 3 ingredients in small bowl; mix well. Drain all fruit. Mix fruit in casserole. Add ginger; sprinkle with brown sugar. Top with curry mixture. Bake at 375 degrees for 30 minutes. Remove ginger.

Mrs. James H. Bryan
Harrisonburg, Virginia

Nectarine Sundae Pudding

1 c. sugar
1 c. flour
1 tsp. salt
½ tsp. soda
¾ c. milk
½ c. butter
1 c. molasses
4 eggs, beaten
½ c. coarsely chopped walnuts

Mix sugar, flour, salt and soda in bowl. Heat milk and butter in saucepan until butter melts. Add with molasses to sugar mixture; beat well. Stir eggs and walnuts into batter. Pour into

buttered 1½-quart casserole. Bake at 350 degrees for 50 minutes or until toothpick inserted in center comes out clean. Serve warm with ice cream and hot Nectarine Sauce.

Nectarine Sauce

3½ tbsp. cornstarch
1 c. sugar
¼ tsp. ground cloves
¼ c. lemon juice
2 tbsp. butter
1½ c. thinly sliced nectarines

Blend cornstarch, sugar and cloves with 1 cup water in saucepan. Cook over medium heat until thick, stirring constantly. Stir in remaining ingredients. Heat for 1 minute longer.

Picture for this recipe on page 111.

Peachy Crumb Cobbler

1 pkg. wild blueberry muffin mix
¾ c. sugar
1½ tsp. cinnamon
¾ stick butter
½ c. chopped pecans
2 cans peach pie filling
3 tsp. almond extract

Drain blueberries; set aside. Combine dry muffin mix, ½ cup sugar and ½ teaspoon cinnamon in bowl. Cut in butter until crumbly; stir in pecans. Combine pie filling, almond extract, blueberries, remaining sugar and cinnamon in 13 × 19-inch baking dish. Spoon crumb topping over filling. Bake at 350 degrees for 30 minutes or until brown.

Nona Pratt
Portland, Oregon

Quick Peach Pie

1 c. sugar
2 c. self-rising flour
1 c. milk
½ c. butter
1 can sliced peaches

Combine sugar, flour and milk in bowl; beat until smooth. Melt butter in baking dish. Spoon half the batter into baking dish. Add peaches and juice. Top with remaining batter. Bake at 350 degrees for 45 minutes.

Winona L. Walker
Baker, Florida

Fresh Peach Cobbler

½ c. butter
1 c. flour
2 tsp. baking powder
1½ c. sugar
¾ c. milk
4 or 5 lg. fresh peaches, peeled, sliced

Melt butter in baking dish. Combine next 3 ingredients with 1 cup sugar in bowl; mix well. Spoon into baking dish. Arrange peach slices over batter. Sprinkle with remaining sugar. Drizzle ½ cup water over peaches. Bake at 350 degrees for 50 minutes or until brown.

Mrs. James Hilderbrand
Mena, Arkansas

Quick Peach Cobbler

1 c. flour
1 c. sugar
3 tsp. baking powder
1 stick margarine
1 lg. can sliced peaches

Combine first 3 ingredients in bowl; mix well. Drain peaches, reserving juice. Add enough water to reserved juice to measure ⅔ cup liquid. Add to flour mixture; mix well. Melt butter in baking dish. Pour batter over butter. Arrange peaches over batter. Bake at 350 degrees for 45 minutes or until brown.

Mona Faye Fordham
Sikes, Louisiana

Mary Ellen's Mixed Fruit Casserole

1 No. 2 can crushed pineapple
1 can cherry pie filling
1 box yellow cake mix
½ to 1 c. chopped pecans
1 stick butter, thinly sliced

Layer pineapple, pie filling, dry cake mix and pecans in 9 × 13-inch baking dish. Do not stir. Cover with butter slices. Bake at 350 degrees for 1 hour.

Mary Ellen Weiss
San Antonio, Texas

Pineapple-Pecan Casserole

1 No. 2 can crushed pineapple
1 box yellow cake mix
2 sticks margarine, sliced
1 c. pecans

Spread pineapple in 9 × 13-inch baking dish. Cover with dry cake mix. Cover with margarine. Top with pecans. Bake at 325 degrees for 25 minutes or until brown. Yield: 15 servings.

Evelyn Coleman
Wynnewood, Oklahoma

Pineapple Crisp

4 c. thinly sliced, pared apples
3 c. diced canned pineapple
1 tbsp. lemon juice
¾ c. packed brown sugar
¼ c. melted butter
½ tsp. cinnamon
¼ tsp. salt
1½ c. crushed cornflakes

Alternate layers of apples and pineapple in 1½-quart casserole. Sprinkle with lemon juice. Combine remaining ingredients in bowl; mix well. Spread over fruit. Bake, covered, at 350 degrees for 30 minutes. Uncover. Bake for 15 minutes longer or until apples are tender. Yield: 6 servings.

Dorothy F. Winsett
Mt. Pleasant, Texas

Royal Rhubarb Crisp

4 c. chopped rhubarb
¾ c. sugar
2 tbsp. quick-cooking tapioca
½ tsp. salt
1 11-oz. can mandarin orange segments, drained
1 c. rolled oats
¼ c. sifted flour
⅓ c. packed brown sugar
¼ c. melted butter

Combine rhubarb, sugar, tapioca and salt in bowl; toss lightly to mix. Let stand for 30 minutes, stirring occasionally. Stir in orange segments. Place in 8-inch baking pan. Combine oats, flour, brown sugar and butter in bowl; mix well. Sprinkle over rhubarb mixture. Bake in 350-degree oven for 40 to 45 minutes. Serve warm with ice cream.

Corinne Rasmussen
Burt, Iowa

Sweet Potato Dessert Casserole

2 eggs
½ c. milk
¾ c. sugar
1 c. margarine, softened
1 can sweet potatoes, drained, mashed
1 tsp. vanilla extract
½ c. flour
½ c. packed brown sugar
½ c. chopped nuts

Place eggs, milk, sugar and half the margarine in blender container. Process for 1 minute. Add potatoes gradually; blend well. Add vanilla; blend. Pour into greased casserole. Mix flour, remaining margarine and brown sugar in small bowl until crumbly; stir in nuts. Sprinkle over potato mixture. Bake in 375-degree oven for 20 to 25 minutes. Yield: 6-8 servings.

Ruth Jordan
Alexander City, Alabama

Coconut Custard

3 eggs, slightly beaten
¼ c. sugar
¼ tsp. salt
2 c. milk, scalded
½ tsp. vanilla extract
Nutmeg to taste
1 c. coconut

Combine first 3 ingredients in bowl; mix well. Add milk slowly, stirring constantly. Stir in remaining ingredients. Pour into custard cups. Place in pan with 1-inch hot water. Bake at 325 degrees for 30 to 40 minutes or until knife inserted in center comes out clean.

Betty Kirschten
Rosebud, Montana

Easy Custard Pie

2 c. milk
4 eggs
¼ c. butter, softened
1 tsp. vanilla extract
½ c. honey
½ c. whole wheat flour
¼ tsp. salt
¼ tsp. nutmeg
1 c. unsweetened coconut

Combine all ingredients in blender container; blend until well mixed. Pour into buttered deep 9-inch pie pan. Bake at 350 degrees for 45 minutes. Makes its own crust.

Linda K. Weber
Boone, Iowa

Rhubarb Custard

2 c. sugar
1½ c. flour
2 qt. diced rhubarb
3 eggs, beaten
2 c. half and half
1 c. packed brown sugar
½ c. butter

Sprinkle sugar and ½ cup flour over rhubarb in 9 × 13-inch baking dish. Beat eggs and half and half together in bowl; pour over rhubarb. Bake at 350 degrees for 30 minutes. Combine brown sugar and remaining flour in bowl. Cut in butter until crumbly. Sprinkle over top. Bake for 30 minutes longer. Yield: 10-12 servings.

Phyllis Pope
Medford, Wisconsin

Old-Time Bread Pudding

4 slices buttered toast, quartered
⅓ c. seedless raisins
2 slightly beaten eggs
Sugar
⅛ tsp. salt
1 c. evaporated milk
1 tsp. vanilla extract
¼ tsp. cinnamon

Place toast in greased 1¼-quart baking dish. Sprinkle with raisins. Combine eggs, ¼ cup sugar, salt, milk, 1 cup boiling water and vanilla in bowl; mix well. Pour over toast. Let stand for 10 minutes. Sprinkle with 4 tablespoons sugar and cinnamon. Bake at 350 degrees for 30 minutes or until knife inserted in center comes out clean. Yield: 4 servings.

Madge C. Young
Taylorsville, North Carolina

NOTES

SIMPLE SAUCES

Miraculously transform meat, fish or poultry into a masterpiece just by adding a simple sauce! Basic savory sauces are few in number, but their variations are almost limitless when spices, herbs or seasonings are added. Here are some quick sauces using creamed soups as a base—so easy for today's busy cooks.

JIFFY SAUCE	SOUP BASE	HOW TO DO IT
Cheese	Cream of celery, chicken or mushroom	Mix 3 tbsp. milk with ½ cup Cheddar cheese; season to taste.
Mock Hollandaise	Cream of celery, chicken or mushroom	Mix ¼ cup mayonnaise with 3 tbsp. water and 3 tsp. lemon juice; season to taste.
Mushroom	Cream of mushroom	Mix with chopped, fresh mushrooms; season to taste.
Peppery Cheese	Cheddar cheese	Mix with cayenne pepper and Tabasco sauce to taste.
Sour Cream	Cream of celery, chicken or mushroom	Mix with ½ cup sour cream. Add milk, if needed; season to taste.
Tomato	Tomato	Saute onions and green peppers. Add a dash of Worcestershire sauce for extra flavor; season to taste.

TIP TOP TOPPINGS

Garnishing your casserole gives it a special "company" look that somehow makes it taste even better! But don't think you have to be traditional. Try these tasty toppings on your next casserole and create a brand new recipe!

—Corn Bread
—Mashed Potatoes
—Toasted Wheat Germ
—Pretzel Crumbs
—Dry Stuffing Mix
—Pastry Cutouts

—Chow Mein Noodles
—French-Fried Onion Rings
—Corn or Potato Chips
—Sesame Seeds or Toasted Nuts
—Green Pepper Rings, Snipped Parsley
—For a different twist, after baking, top with lemon or avocado slices

---

Making Your Own Bread Crumb Topping

Here's a great casserole topper that's easy and economical to prepare: Toast stale bread in a 300-degree oven until crisp. Then crush in a blender or with a rolling pin. Toss with seasonings such as Parmesan cheese, oregano, curry, lemon peel, sage or thyme. One slice of bread = approximately ¼ cup crumbs.

Ingredient Equivalents

	WHEN RECIPE CALLS FOR:	YOU NEED:
BREAD & CEREAL	1 c. soft bread crumbs	2 slices
	1 c. fine dry bread crumbs	4-5 slices
	1 c. small bread cubes	2 slices
	1 c. fine cracker crumbs	24 saltines
	1 c. fine graham cracker crumbs	14 crackers
	1 c. vanilla wafer crumbs	22 wafers
	1 c. crushed corn flakes	3 c. uncrushed
	4 c. cooked macaroni	1 8-oz. package
	3½ c. cooked rice	1 c. uncooked
DAIRY	1 c. freshly grated cheese	¼ lb.
	1 c. cottage cheese or sour cream	1 8-oz. carton
	⅔ c. evaporated milk	1 sm. can
	1⅔ c. evaporated milk	1 tall can
	1 c. whipped cream	½ c. heavy cream
FRUIT	4 c. sliced or chopped apples	4 medium
	2 c. pitted cherries	4 c. unpitted
	3 to 4 tbsp. lemon juice plus 1 tsp. grated peel	1 lemon
	⅓ c. orange juice plus 2 tsp. grated peel	1 orange
	1 c. mashed banana	3 medium
	4 c. cranberries	1 lb.
	3 c. shredded coconut	½ lb.
	4 c. sliced peaches	8 medium
	1 c. pitted dates or candied fruit	1 8-oz. package
	2 c. pitted prunes	1 12-oz. package
	3 c. raisins	1 15-oz. package
MEAT	3 c. diced cooked meat	1 lb., cooked
	2 c. ground cooked meat	1 lb., cooked
	4 c. diced cooked chicken	1 5-lb. chicken
NUTS	1 c. chopped nuts	4 oz. shelled
		1 lb. unshelled
VEGETABLES	4 c. sliced or diced raw potatoes	4 medium
	2 c. cooked green beans	½ lb. fresh or 1 16-oz. can
	1 c. chopped onion	1 large
	4 c. shredded cabbage	1 lb.
	2 c. canned tomatoes	1 16-oz. can
	1 c. grated carrot	1 large
	2½ c. lima beans or red beans	1 c. dried, cooked
	1 4-oz. can mushrooms	½ lb. fresh

Measurement Equivalents

1 tbsp. = 3 tsp.	4 qt. = 1 gal.
2 tbsp. = 1 oz.	6½ to 8-oz. can = 1 c.
4 tbsp. = ¼ oz.	10½ to 12-oz. can = 1¼ c.
5 tbsp. + 1 tsp. = ⅓ c.	14 to 16-oz. can (No. 300) = 1¾ c.
8 tbsp. = ½ c.	16 to 17-oz. can (No. 303) = 2 c.
12 tbsp. = ¾ c.	1-lb. 4-oz. can or 1-pt. 2-oz. can (No. 2) = 2½ c.
16 tbsp. = 1 c.	1-lb. 13-oz. can (No. 2½) = 3½ c.
1 c. = 8 oz. or ½ pt.	3-lb. 3-oz. can or 46-oz. can or 1-qt. 14-oz. can = 5¾ c.
4 c. = 1 qt.	6½-lb. or 7-lb. 5-oz. can (No. 10) = 12 to 13 c.

Measurement Abbreviations

Cup..c.	Large...lg.
Tablespoon.............................tbsp.	Package..pkg.
Teaspoon................................ tsp.	Square..sq.
Pound.................................... lb.	Dozen..doz.
Ounce.................................... oz.	Pint.. pt.
Gallon....................................gal.	Quart.. qt.

Metric Conversion Chart

VOLUME

1 tsp.	=	4.9 cc
1 tbsp.	=	14.7 cc
⅓ c.	=	28.9 cc
⅛ c.	=	29.5 cc
¼ c.	=	59.1 cc
½ c.	=	118.3 cc
¾ c.	=	177.5 cc
1 c.	=	236.7 cc
2 c.	=	473.4 cc
1 fl. oz.	=	29.5 cc
4 oz.	=	118.3 cc
8 oz.	=	236.7 cc

1 pt.	=	473.4 cc
1 qt.	=	.946 liters
1 gal.	=	3.7 liters

CONVERSION FACTORS:

Liters	×	1.056 = Liquid quarts
Quarts	×	0.946 = Liters
Liters	×	0.264 = Gallons
Gallons	×	3.785 = Liters
Fluid ounces	×	29.563 = Cubic centimeters
Cubic centimeters	×	0.034 = Fluid ounces
Cups	×	236.575 = Cubic centimeters
Tablespoons	×	14.797 = Cubic centimeters
Teaspoons	×	4.932 = Cubic centimeters
Bushels	×	0.352 = Hectoliters
Hectoliters	×	2.837 = Bushels

WEIGHT

1 dry oz.	=	28.3 Grams
1 lb.	=	.454 Kilograms

CONVERSION FACTORS:

Ounces (Avoir.)	×	28.349 = Grams
Grams	×	0.035 = Ounces
Pounds	×	0.454 = Kilograms
Kilograms	×	2.205 = Pounds

INDEX

PHOTOGRAPHY CREDITS:

Cover: Tuna Research Foundation; National Macaroni Institute; American Dairy Association; The McIlhenny Company; National Dairy Council; R. T. French Company; Louisiana Yam Commission; Green Giant Company; General Foods Kitchens; International Shrimp Council; National Kraut Packers Association; Spanish Green Olive Commission; Ralston Purina Company; Quaker Oats; United Fresh Fruit and Vegetable Association; and Fresh California Nectarines.

Favorite Recipes ®
of Home Economics Teachers
COOKBOOKS

Add to
Your Cookbook Collection
Select from These ALL-TIME
Favorites

BOOK TITLE	ITEM NUMBER
Casseroles (1982) 128 pages	18295
Today's All-Purpose Cookbook (1982) 168 Pages	15717
Holiday Season Cookbook (1981) 160 Pages	15040
Breads (1981) 128 Pages	15032
Meats (1981) 128 Pages	14958
*Salads * Vegetables* (1979) 200 Pages	05576
Desserts—Revised Edition (1962) 304 Pages	01422
Quick and Easy Dishes—Revised Edition (1968) 256 Pages	00043
Dieting To Stay Fit (1978) 200 Pages	01449
Foods From Foreign Nations (1977) 200 Pages	01279
Life-Saver Cookbook (1976) 200 Pages	70335
Canning, Preserving and Freezing (1975) 200 Pages	70084
Americana Cooking (1972) 192 Pages	70351

FOR ORDERING INFORMATION
Write to:
Favorite Recipes Press
P. O. Box 77
Nashville, Tennessee 37202

BOOKS OFFERED SUBJECT TO AVAILABILITY.